Masteri MAKE

A Guide to Building Programs
on DOS and UNIX® Systems

Clovis L. Tondo
International Business Machines Corporation

Center for Computer and Information Sciences
Nova University, Ft. Lauderdale, Florida

Andrew Nathanson
Beneficial Data Processing Corporation
Peapack, New Jersey

Eden Yount
Modular Computer Systems, Incorporated
Ft. Lauderdale, Florida

P T R Prentice Hall
Englewood Cliffs, New Jersey 07632

Library of Congress Cataloging-in-Publication Data

Tondo, Clovis L.
    Mastering MAKE : a guide to building programs on DOS and UNIX
  systems / Clovis L. Tondo, Andrew Nathanson, Eden Yount.
        p.   cm.
    Includes bibliographical references and index.
    ISBN 0-13-554619-2
    1. Utilities (Computer programs) 2. Computer software-
  -Development--Management.   I. Nathanson, Andrew. II. Yount, Eden.
  III. Title.
  QA76.76.U84T66 1992
  005.1--dc20   91-39867
                                                              CIP

Editorial/production supervision: Mary P. Rottino
Cover design: Lundgren Graphics
Cover illustration: Ken Scanllon (Image Bank)
Manufacturing buyer: Susan Brunke
Pre-press buyer: Mary E. McCartney
Acquisitions editor: Greg Doench

© 1992 by P T R Prentice-Hall, Inc.
A Simon & Schuster Company
Englewood Cliffs, New Jersey 07632

The publisher offers discounts on this book when ordered
in bulk quantities. For more information, write:

> Special Sales/Professional Marketing
> Prentice-Hall, Inc.
> Professional & Technical Reference Division
> Englewood Cliffs, New Jersey 07632

IBM is a trademark of International Business Machines Corporation. MS-DOS and Microsoft C are
trademarks of Microsoft Corporation. TURBO C and TURBO C++ are trademarks of Borland
International. UNIX is a registered trademark of UNIX System Laboratories, Inc. L^AT_EX is a
trademark of Addison-Wesley. PCT_EX is a trademark of Personal T_EX, Inc. T_EX is a trademark of
the American Mathematical Society.

This book was typeset by the authors using L^AT_EX and PCT_EX and was printed with the Chelgraph
IBX typesetter by TYPE 2000, 16 Madrona Avenue, Mill Valley, CA 94941.

Printed in the United States of America
10 9 8 7 6 5 4 3

ISBN 0-13-554619-2

Prentice-Hall International (UK) Limited, *London*
Prentice-Hall of Australia Pty. Limited, *Sydney*
Prentice-Hall Canada Inc., *Toronto*
Prentice-Hall Hispanoamericana, S.A., *Mexico*
Prentice-Hall of India Private Limited, *New Delhi*
Prentice-Hall of Japan, Inc., *Tokyo*
Simon & Schuster Asia Pte. Ltd., *Singapore*
Editora Prentice-Hall do Brasil, Ltda., *Rio de Janeiro*

Contents

Preface   vii

1 Fundamentals of MAKE   **1**
   1.1 The Theory Behind MAKE   2
   1.2 The Makefile   2
      1.2.1 Syntax Rules   2
      1.2.2 Targets   3
      1.2.3 Dependencies   5
   1.3 MAKE Operations   6
   1.4 Summary   8

2 Invoking MAKE   **11**
   2.1 Common MAKE Options   11
   2.2 Examples   12
   2.3 Using Hard-Coded Commands   13
   2.4 Using Commands with Macros   14
   2.5 More About Dependencies   17
   2.6 Summary   19

3 More About MAKE   **21**
   3.1 More About Macros   21
      3.1.1 User-Defined Macros   22
      3.1.2 Predefined Macros   23
      3.1.3 Macros and the p Option   26
   3.2 Pseudotargets   26
      3.2.1 User-Defined Pseudotargets   26
      3.2.2 Predefined Pseudotargets   27
   3.3 Inference Rules and Implicit Commands   28

      3.3.1   User-Defined Inference Rules 30

      3.3.2   Predefined Inference Rules 33

  3.4 How Are We Doing? 35

  3.5 Application: Makefile for Text Formatting 37

  3.6 Summary 38

4 Advanced Topics   **43**

  4.1 Using MAKE Recursively 43

  4.2 Using Environment Variables in Makefiles 51

  4.3 DOS: Input Files and In-Line Response Files 56

  4.4 Common Errors 59

  4.5 Summary 62

5 Microsoft's NMAKE   **65**

  5.1 Invoking NMAKE 65

  5.2 Command Line Options 65

  5.3 Preprocessing Directives 67

  5.4 Special Cases 72

  5.5 Creating Dependencies Dynamically 73

  5.6 NMAKE and the tools.ini File 78

  5.7 Macro Precedence 79

  5.8 Summary 79

6 Borland's MAKE   **81**

  6.1 Invoking MAKE 81

  6.2 Command Line Options 81

  6.3 Preprocessing Directives 83

  6.4 Continuation Lines 90

  6.5 Creating Dependencies Dynamically 91

  6.6 MAKE and the builtins.mak File 93

  6.7 Macro Precedence 95

  6.8 Summary 95

7 UNIX System's MAKE   **97**

  7.1 Invoking MAKE 97

  7.2 Command Line Options 97

  7.3 Makefile Command Lines 98

  7.4 Environment Variables 99

  7.5 Macros and Macro Precedence 100

7.6   Suffixes and Inference Rules 101

7.7   Summary 103

A Comparing MAKE   **105**

B Microsoft's NMAKE   **107**

C Borland's MAKE   **111**

D UNIX System's MAKE   **113**

E Depends Utility   **115**

Index   **137**

Preface

The purpose of this book is to help you, as a programmer, understand and use the *make* utility. If you spend much of your time, as we do, in a software development environment, you probably are well aware of the need for a tool such as *make*. If you are just entering this challenging arena — or are drawn by simple curiosity — you soon will appreciate the value of this utility.

It has been our experience that a good many programmers have heard of, and even worked with, the *make* utility without ever understanding exactly what it does or why they are (or should be) using it. And while many programmers write makefiles that work, they do not exploit the full power of the tool. Others (including even veteran programmers) struggle along in the too common, mostly unproductive trial-and-error process of trying to learn how to use *make* effectively. And they enjoy little success for their efforts.

Other than the usual manuals and online help files that come with a DOS compiler or a UNIX system, there is a paucity of information available about this invaluable tool. What is available seems directed to a narrow audience and intended primarily as reference material, without offering much in the way of guidance to the uninitiated.

Mastering MAKE is our effort to fill this void:

- to explain how *make* works

- to suggest reasons for using it

- to demonstrate its versatility and flexibility in a variety of real-life applications

- to provide a smooth, logical progression for learning the utility from its basic concepts to its most sophisticated implementations

In short, to share with you what we've learned.

We approached this project with the idea of writing a book that would benefit a wide audience. We wanted to address the needs of less experienced programmers while augmenting the knowledge already acquired by more experienced software developers.

At the same time, we did not want to limit our discussion to a single version of *make*. Long established on UNIX systems, the *make* utility is available — though perhaps less widely known or used — on other operating systems as well. We wanted to cover not only universal features of *make*, but also those that apply specifically to particular operating systems: namely, DOS and UNIX systems.

It was a challenge that we set for ourselves, but one that we believe we have met.

We have selected three versions of *make* around which to develop both general principles and specific applications. These versions are:

- NMAKE from Microsoft

  The **nmake** command is part of the C Compiler, Version 6.0A package from Microsoft. It is a relatively new command and is not part of any previous C language product from Microsoft.

- MAKE from Borland

  The **make** command is part of the Turbo C++ Compiler, Version 2.0, which (at the time of writing) is the latest of the Turbo C++ packages from Borland.

- MAKE for UNIX systems

  The **make** command is part of UNIX systems. Examples in this book identified for use on UNIX systems have been tested on a system based on UNIX System V.3.

We have used NMAKE from Microsoft (with C version 6.0A) as our baseline version of *make*. Where differences exist for MAKE from Borland or for MAKE on UNIX systems, the variations are identified. Example makefiles are written for use with the **nmake** command, unless specifically stated otherwise.

Of course, we must have some common ground from which to start. In the present case, we assume you are comfortably familiar with your operating system environment, whether you are working on a DOS or a UNIX system. (However, you are not required to have achieved the status of guru!) We assume also that you have a comfortable working relationship with your compiler. With this foundation, you should be able to progress painlessly through these pages, regardless of your level of experience with software development projects or the *make* utility.

You'll find that *Mastering MAKE* combines elements of both a tutorial and a reference book. With the introduction of each new concept, you will find examples of tested makefiles. You can use these to gain confidence and to test your understanding. At the end of each chapter we review salient concepts. These summaries are useful as reference material, particularly for the more experienced programmers in our audience. We have designed the appendices to serve as convenient quick reference guides; you'll be able to identify effortlessly the features that apply specifically to each version of *make*.

We begin in Chapter 1 with the principal concepts of *make* and introduce the basic elements of a makefile, then build on these in Chapters 2 and 3 in logical, easy-to-follow steps. By the time you reach Chapter 4, you will be ready to take full advantage of the power of *make* as you develop sophisticated makefiles to support practical, real-life applications. At every step, we emphasize good programming practices and the value of developing makefiles that are flexible and easy to maintain.

Beginning with Chapter 5, we look at the specifics of each version of *make*. Chapter 5 is devoted to Microsoft's NMAKE, Chapter 6 to Borland's MAKE, and Chapter 7 to MAKE on UNIX systems.

Inevitably, some of the information in *Mastering MAKE* duplicates information provided in the manuals and online help files that came with your DOS compiler or your UNIX system. *Mastering MAKE* is not meant to supplant that documentation, but to supplement it with tactics and strategies acquired from our combined experiences with the utility. Even those among you who are well-versed in the intricacies of *make* will undoubtedly pick up some subtleties and hints that may have escaped you in the past.

Regardless of your individual starting point, we are confident you will find, at the end, that you have indeed mastered *make*.

Acknowledgements

The writing and publishing of any book is an undertaking that requires the efforts of many people, not just the authors. We have a number of people to whom we owe our appreciation. Jointly, we thank the reviewers, who offered insightful suggestions for improving the book: Richard Fencel, Mary Forlenza, George Gabb, Tom Harvey, Bruce Leung, Carlos Tondo, and an anonymous reviewer. We thank also Jeff Codella, Dave Egan, David Frith, and David Thomas for their help with hardware.

Separately, we owe thanks to individuals who provided support and encouragement to each of us.

Clovis thanks Caren Webster, Klaus Luedtke, Irma Miller, Carl and Sandy Schuster, and Bob Webster for their support.

Andrew thanks Lorraine Patrone, David Hoffman, the Guillets, and Elaine Nathanson and dedicates his efforts to the memory of Joseph Nathanson.

Eden thanks Paula Devereaux and, especially, John Gallipoli, whose patience and sense of humor make all things possible.

Finally, we are grateful to the people at Prentice Hall whose various talents and skills helped guide and shape this project from concept through completion. In particular, we thank Greg Doench, Joan Magrabi, and Mary Rottino without whom *Mastering MAKE* would never have become a reality.

CLT

AN

EY

Chapter 1

Fundamentals of MAKE

The *make* utility was created to help programmers manage software development projects and files associated with those projects. The original version of *make* (created by Stuart I. Feldman) runs on UNIX systems. A few versions of *make* exist for DOS. In this book, we address two versions for DOS — NMAKE by Microsoft and MAKE by Borland — as well as MAKE for UNIX systems.

To understand how *make* operates, let's first discuss the need for such a tool. Here is a typical scenario:

> You are working on a number of programs that will be compiled and linked together to form a single executable program. Every time you change one of the files, you have to recompile that file, then relink it with the existing object files to create a new executable program.

This scenario presents a significant problem: you, the programmer, have to remember which files have been modified and, consequently, which files have to be recompiled. Because you need to remember many details, keeping track of modified files and recompiling them soon become cumbersome, difficult tasks.

The *make* utility handles all the details of compiling the modified files for you. To accomplish the task, *make* follows a set of rules that you provide in a special file called a makefile.

1.1   The Theory Behind MAKE

The theory behind *make* is straightforward: *make* compares the date and time of a source file with the date and time of the associated object file. (Together, the date and time are called the time stamp.) If the comparison shows that the source file is newer than the object file — or if the object file does not exist — *make* performs the tasks you have listed in the makefile to convert the source file into an object file. On the other hand, if the object file is newer than the source file, then *make* recognizes that it does not have to recompile the source file.

1.2   The Makefile

We mentioned earlier that *make* follows a set of rules that you provide in a special file called a makefile. A makefile consists of several elements. Two elements of a makefile are targets and dependencies; we meet them in this chapter. Other elements, such as commands, macro definitions, and inference rules, are covered in later chapters.

1.2.1   Syntax Rules

Here is our first makefile (the example uses Microsoft's C compiler):

```
prog.exe:  prog1.obj  prog2.obj
        cl  -o  prog.exe  prog1.obj  prog2.obj

prog1.obj:  prog1.c
        cl  -c  -W2  -O  prog1.c

prog2.obj:  prog2.c
        cl  -c  -W2  -O  prog2.c
```

We must follow a few rules when we write a makefile. The example we just looked at illustrates the first two rules.

Our makefile consists of three similar pairs of lines. In each set, the first line is a target/dependency line, and the second is a command line. Here are the rules for these types of lines:

1. A target/dependency line must begin in the first column of the line.

2. A command line must be indented.

The requirements for indenting a command line vary depending on the version of *make*. With the two DOS versions, we can use blank spaces or tabs; one blank space or one tab is the required minimum. MAKE on UNIX systems requires a tab — and not spaces — at the beginning of the command line.

Our first makefile is very simple. We'll see later, in more complex examples, instances in which a list of dependencies or a command is so long that it does not fit on one line but must be carried over to a second line — or more.

This situation gives us our third syntax rule:

3. We must use a backslash (\) at the end of a line to tell *make* that the next line is a continuation of the current line.

We can also use continuation lines to enhance the readability of the makefile. We will see this technique in practice in later examples.

Good coding practice applies as much to the makefiles we write as to any other type of program we develop. This means that, except for very simple cases (such as our first example), we should include comments to explain the purpose of individual lines or groups of lines in a makefile. Our fourth syntax rule applies to comments in a makefile:

4. We must use a pound sign (#) to tell *make* that what follows is a comment and not a makefile statement to be acted on.

We can put a comment on a line by itself, or we can put it on a line that *make* executes. When we put a comment on a line by itself, the pound sign can be anywhere on the line, although common practice is to put it in the first column. When we put a comment on the same line as an executable makefile statement, the comment goes at the end of the line; that is, the pound sign follows the makefile statement and everything that follows the pound sign is considered to be a comment, which *make* ignores.

Comment lines cannot be continued with the backslash character. However, we can write multiple comment lines anywhere in the makefile so long as we start each comment with a pound sign.

1.2.2 Targets

A target is a name followed by a colon (:). The name appears at the beginning of a line. (The other names on the line are called dependencies.

We will tell you about dependencies a little later.)

A name that begins with a dot (.) and ends with a colon looks like a target, but it is not. These are called inference rules or suffix rules. We will tell you more about inference rules in Chapter 3.

In our makefile, the first line

```
prog.exe:  prog1.obj  prog2.obj
```

begins with the target `prog.exe`. Our makefile has two more targets. The third line

```
prog1.obj:  prog1.c
```

begins with the target `prog1.obj`. And on the fifth line

```
prog2.obj:  prog2.c
```

the target is `prog2.obj`.

The default is for *make* to build the first target in the makefile. When we enter

```
nmake
```

make understands that we want to build the target `prog.exe`. (Use `make`, instead of `nmake`, if you are using Borland's MAKE or MAKE on a UNIX system.)

We can tell *make* explicitly which target we want to build by issuing, for example:

```
nmake  prog.exe
```

This command is equivalent to the plain `nmake` command we just looked at because `prog.exe` is the first target in the makefile. Unless we tell it otherwise, *make* builds the first target.

Here is another example:

```
nmake  prog2.obj
```

This command tells *make* to build only the target `prog2.obj`. In this case, *make* concerns itself only with these lines of our makefile:

```
prog2.obj:  prog2.c
        cl  -c  -W2  -O  prog2.c
```

The target `prog2.obj` depends on `prog2.c`. If `prog2.c` is newer than `prog2.obj`, or if `prog2.obj` does not exist, *make* issues the command

```
cl  -c  -W2  -O  prog2.c
```

which builds the target `prog2.obj`. Then *make* stops because no other dependencies are associated with the target `prog2.obj`.

Each target can have its own set of one or more explicit commands; that is, commands that appear explicitly with the target to which they apply. Later on, when we tell you about suffix rules, we also will tell you about implicit commands.

1.2.3 Dependencies

Two types of dependencies occur in a makefile: direct dependencies and indirect dependencies.

A direct dependency appears with the target. This means the target depends on the file or files listed after the colon.

In our makefile, the target, `prog.exe`, has two direct dependencies, `prog1.obj` and `prog2.obj`:

```
prog.exe:  prog1.obj  prog2.obj
```

The direct dependency `prog1.obj`, in turn, depends on another file:

```
prog1.obj:  prog1.c
```

`prog1.c` is a direct dependency for the target `prog1.obj`. The file `prog1.obj` is a direct dependency for `prog.exe`. Consequently, `prog1.c` is an indirect dependency for `prog.exe`.

An indirect dependency is indirectly related to the first target.

Let's look again at our makefile example for a clearer understanding of direct and indirect dependencies. If we draw out the order of precedence, we end up with a tree that shows the dependencies for the target `prog.exe`. See Figure 1.1 to observe how *make* views the dependencies.

The first target `prog.exe` depends directly on the files `prog1.obj` and `prog2.obj`. `prog1.obj` depends directly on `prog1.c`, and `prog2.obj` depends directly on `prog2.c`. The target `prog.exe` then depends indirectly on `prog1.c` and `prog2.c`.

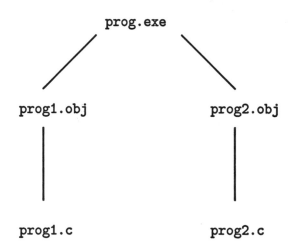

Figure 1.1: Dependency Tree

1.3   MAKE Operations

The usual way to invoke *make* is to issue the command **nmake** (or **make** with Borland's software or on a UNIX system) at the operating system prompt. *make* then searches for a makefile in the current directory; the default name of the makefile is **makefile**. If *make* cannot find this file, it issues a message like:

Make: No arguments or description file. Stop

In our case, *make* finds the makefile. It is our first makefile (from page 2); here it is again:

```
prog.exe:  prog1.obj  prog2.obj
        cl  -o  prog.exe  prog1.obj  prog2.obj

prog1.obj:  prog1.c
        cl  -c  -W2  -O  prog1.c

prog2.obj:  prog2.c
        cl  -c  -W2  -O  prog2.c
```

Because we issued a plain **nmake** command, the target that *make* is going to build is the first target in the makefile; specifically, **prog.exe**.

make sees that `prog1.obj` is a dependency for that target, so it compares the date and time of the object file `prog1.obj` with the date and time of its dependency, `prog1.c`. If `prog1.obj` is older than `prog1.c`, then *make* uses the makefile command

```
cl  -c  -W2  -O  prog1.c
```

to invoke the C compiler and produce a new `prog1.obj`. On the other hand, if `prog1.obj` is newer than `prog1.c`, then *make* understands that `prog1.obj` was created after the last time `prog1.c` was modified. In this case, *make* does not issue any command because `prog1.c` does not have to be recompiled.

    make then checks the date and time of `prog2.obj` and `prog2.c` to determine if `prog2.c` needs to be recompiled.

    When all the object files (`.obj` files) are up-to-date with respect to their source files, *make* examines the date and time of `prog.exe` and the date and time of each of the `.obj` files that we told *make* are necessary to produce the executable file (`.exe` file). In our example, *make* knows which object files to look at from the first line of the makefile:

```
prog.exe:  prog1.obj  prog2.obj
```

If any `.obj` file is newer than the `.exe` file, then *make* issues the command

```
cl  -o  prog.exe  prog1.obj  prog2.obj
```

to link `prog1.obj`, `prog2.obj`, and the necessary functions from the default C library to produce `prog.exe`. (The compiler command we use — in this case, `cl` — determines which C library will be linked in with our object files.) If all of the `.obj` files are older than the `.exe` file, then *make* does nothing; it has completed its work.

    If we use Borland's C compiler, the name of the compiler command we use in the makefile is different. To invoke the compiler, we use `tcc` (instead of `cl`). This means our makefile would look like this:

```
prog.exe:  prog1.obj  prog2.obj
        tcc  -eprog.exe  prog1.obj  prog2.obj

prog1.obj:  prog1.c
        tcc  -c  -O  prog1.c

prog2.obj:  prog2.c
        tcc  -c  -O  prog2.c
```

1.4 Summary

make is a utility that simplifies the problem of keeping track of modified files and recompiling and relinking those files to produce an executable program. *make* works by following rules that we provide in a makefile.

make requires us to follow certain rules when we write a makefile. The basic rules are:

1. We must start a target/dependency line in the first column of the line.

2. We must indent a command line, using one or more blank spaces or tabs. (The DOS versions of *make* accept either means of indenting the line; the UNIX version requires a tab.)

3. We must use a backslash (\) at the end of a line that is to be carried over to the next line.

4. We must use a pound sign (#) to tell *make* that what follows is a comment. A comment can begin anywhere on a line. We can write any number of comment lines, each beginning with a pound sign, but we cannot use the backslash to indicate the continuation of a comment.

Two of the basic elements of a makefile are targets and dependencies. *make* works by comparing the time stamp of each target and its dependencies. It recompiles a source file only if the source file is newer than its associated object file.

We can tailor the operation of *make* by specifying a target when we issue the **nmake** command. Here are two examples of **nmake** commands:

```
nmake
```

runs *make* on a makefile that appears in the current directory.

    nmake   target

runs *make* on `target` only. When we do not specify a target, *make* builds the first target in the makefile.

Chapter 2

Invoking MAKE

make is invoked interactively from the command line of the operating system. For example, if we are using DOS and the prompt is

    C>

we invoke Microsoft's *make* by typing `nmake` after the prompt:

    C> nmake

We invoke Borland's *make* by typing `make` after the prompt:

    C> make

The *make* utility searches the current directory for a file called `makefile`.

In Chapter 1, we saw how *make* works when we issue a plain `make` command (as we just did), and we saw the effect of invoking *make* with a target. We can control other details of the operation of *make* by issuing various command line options with the *make* command.

2.1 Common MAKE Options

We can invoke *make* with many different options. Although the actual options and what they do vary among the different versions of *make*, they all have some characteristics in common. (In Chapters 5, 6, and 7 we will tell you about the options that apply specifically to NMAKE by Microsoft, MAKE by Borland, and UNIX MAKE.) In all versions, an option is represented by a single character (sometimes called a flag) preceded by either a dash (-) or a forward slash (/). UNIX and DOS use the dash; a forward slash is used only in DOS.

Here are some of the options we can use with *make*:

f *filename*   Use *filename* instead of the default name of `makefile`. Note that Borland's MAKE expects the file name to follow the flag without any intervening spaces (e.g., f*filename*).

n   Go through the makefile without executing any of the commands. This option is helpful in debugging a makefile.

p   Print all macros and target information.

We can use as many options as we like with the *make* command, and we can invoke *make* with options and a target. The target must be the last item on the command line.

Refer to Chapters 5, 6, and 7 for a list of other options available for NMAKE by Microsoft, MAKE by Borland, and UNIX MAKE.

2.2   Examples

In Chapter 1 we created a makefile and called it `makefile`. We chose to name our file `makefile` because *make* automatically searches for `makefile`. But we can direct *make* to search for a makefile that has any name. We do that by using the **f** option followed by a file name. For example, assume we rename our makefile to be `prog1.mak`. Now we have to tell *make* that our makefile is `prog1.mak`:

```
nmake  -f  prog1.mak
```

Remember that Borland's *make* expects the file name to follow **-f** without any intervening spaces, so the command would be:

```
make  -fprog1.mak
```

If we want *make* just to tell us what must be done to create the first target in the makefile, without actually performing the task(s), we use the **n** option:

```
nmake  -n
```

make searches for `makefile`, checks the date and time of targets and dependencies, and reports the necessary actions. To do this, *make* displays each line it would have to execute to build the target. For example, using the makefile that appears in Section 1.2 and again in Section 2.3, when the `.obj` and `.exe` files have not yet been generated, NMAKE produces:

```
cl  -c  -W2  -0  prog1.c
cl  -c  -W2  -0  prog2.c
cl  -o prog.exe  prog1  prog2
```

What if the makefile is not `makefile`, but `prog1.mak`? We then use both the **n** option and the **f** option:

```
nmake  -n  -f  prog1.mak
```

or

```
nmake  -f  prog1.mak  -n
```

As you can see, the options in *make* can appear in any order. Notice one important restriction: when we use the **f** option, the name of the makefile must immediately follow the flag. (And in Borland's *make*, we cannot have any blank spaces between **-f** and the makefile name.)

2.3   Using Hard-Coded Commands

We introduced makefiles in Chapter 1. Recall that a makefile contains the rules that *make* uses to build an executable object. In addition to targets and dependencies, the rules in a makefile include commands. We are not limited to one command per target; we can use as many commands as we want. And we can write the commands in a makefile in one of two ways: we can hard-code them, or we can use macros on the command line.

The makefile we used in Chapter 1 had information about what to compile and what to link to produce the target `prog.exe`. Here is that makefile again:

```
prog.exe:  prog1.obj  prog2.obj
        cl  -o  prog.exe  prog1.obj  prog2.obj

prog1.obj:  prog1.c
        cl  -c  -W2  -O  prog1.c

prog2.obj:  prog2.c
        cl  -c  -W2  -O  prog2.c
```

In this makefile, **prog.exe** is the target and **prog1.obj** and **prog2.obj** are the dependencies. That means, **prog.exe** depends on **prog1.obj** and **prog2.obj**.

Notice that each dependency item has a command associated with it. In these lines

```
prog1.obj:  prog1.c
        cl  -c  -W2  -O  prog1.c
```

prog1.c is the dependency and the command associated with it is:

```
cl  -c  -W2  -O  prog1.c
```

This is an example of a hard-coded command: it is an explicit, literal command that appears with the target **prog1.obj** (which is a dependency for **prog.exe**).

We can hard-code as many commands for the target as we want. For example, we can echo a message before compiling the file **prog1.c**:

```
prog1.obj:  prog1.c
        echo  Compiling  prog1.c
        cl  -c  -W2  -O  prog1.c
```

2.4 Using Commands with Macros

Hard-coded commands are fixed. That means because we used **cl** in **prog1.obj**, *make* will always invoke **cl** whenever it needs to recompile **prog1.c**. However, what happens if we want to use a different compiler?

Remember what we did in Chapter 1 to switch from Microsoft C to Borland's Turbo C? We modified the makefile; specifically, we changed **cl** to **tcc**. We had to repeat the modification in several places. An alternative to making the same change numerous times is to use a macro.

A macro is a makefile variable. We name the macro and assign a value to it. When *make* reads and executes the makefile, the macro is expanded to its assigned value. For example, we used a hard-coded command in `prog1.obj`:

```
prog1.obj:  prog1.c
        cl  -c  -W2  -O  prog1.c
```

As an alternative, we can define a macro to indicate the compiler we want to use:

```
CC = cl
```

Macros usually appear in uppercase so it is easier to discern a macro from a command.

We use $( ) around the macro name when we want *make* to use the value assigned to the macro:

```
prog1.obj:  prog1.c
        $(CC)  -c  -W2  -O  prog1.c
```

At execution time, *make* interprets $(CC) as 'the value assigned to CC.' In this case, the value is `cl`.

We can also define a macro for the compiler options:

```
CFLAGS  =  -c  -W2  -O
```

Using both macros, the command for the target `prog1.obj` then becomes:

```
prog1.obj:  prog1.c
        $(CC)  $(CFLAGS)  prog1.c
```

Now the makefile looks like this:

```
CC      =  cl
CFLAGS  =  -c  -W2  -O

prog.exe:  prog1.obj  prog2.obj
        $(CC)  -o prog.exe  prog1  prog2

prog1.obj:  prog1.c
        $(CC)  $(CFLAGS)  prog1.c

prog2.obj:  prog2.c
        $(CC)  $(CFLAGS)  prog2.c
```

What if we choose to use Borland's C compiler instead of Microsoft's C compiler? When we use macros consistently in a makefile we have to change only the macros:

```
CC      =  cl
CFLAGS  =  -c  -W2  -O
```

The macros become:

```
CC      =  tcc
CFLAGS  =  -c  -O
```

What if we choose to use the C compiler in a UNIX system? We then change the macros to read:

```
CC      =  cc
CFLAGS  =  -c  -O
```

We also must change the .obj extensions to .o. The rest of the makefile remains the same.

Using macros in a makefile offers several advantages over using hard-coded commands. As we've just seen, macros add flexibility to a makefile because they make it easier to modify the commands. In addition, macros help reduce the possibility for introducing errors: the compiler name and the compiler options appear in one place; if they are not right, we need to correct the error in one place only. *make* uses the identical value for a macro every place we refer to the macro.

A macro can contain any text. Sometimes the macro replacement value is a command, such as cl or tcc; sometimes it is a string that contains a message we want to display during execution. For example, in the following makefile the macros COMMENT1, COMMENT2, and COMMENT3 contain strings that tell us what *make* is doing:

```
CC       = cl
CFLAGS   = -c -W2 -O
COMMENT1 = "Creating prog1.obj file"
COMMENT2 = "Creating prog2.obj file"
COMMENT3 = "Linking prog1.obj and prog2.obj"

prog.exe: prog1.obj  prog2.obj
        echo $(COMMENT3)
        $(CC)  -o  prog.exe  prog1  prog2

prog1.obj:  prog1.c
        echo $(COMMENT1)
        $(CC)  $(CFLAGS)  prog1.c

prog2.obj:  prog2.c
        echo $(COMMENT2)
        $(CC)  $(CFLAGS)  prog2.c
```

As *make* builds each target, we see the following messages:

```
Creating prog1.obj file
Creating prog2.obj file
Linking prog1.obj and prog2.obj
```

2.5 More About Dependencies

A C program, such as prog1.c in our example, usually uses #include to include a file that contains #define statements or C constants that the program requires. In C, these files are called 'include files' or 'header files' and usually have a .h extension.

What if prog1.c contained the line

```
#include   "prog1.h"
```

to include the contents of the file prog1.h? We should state that dependency for the target prog1.obj in our makefile:

```
prog1.obj:  prog1.c  prog1.h
        $(CC)  $(CFLAGS)  prog1.c
```

This means that `prog1.obj` depends on `prog1.c` and `prog1.h`. If either dependency — `prog1.c` or `prog1.h` — has a date or time newer than the date or time of `prog1.obj`, or if `prog1.obj` does not exist yet, then *make* executes the command that follows the target to build `prog1.obj`:

```
$(CC)  $(CFLAGS)  prog1.c
```

The dependency tree for `prog1.obj` appears in Figure 2.1 below.

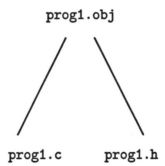

Figure 2.1: Dependency Tree

The dependency tree for `prog.exe` appears in Figure 2.2 on page 19.

You can write a program that automatically builds dependencies for a makefile. We have written one that builds dependencies for a makefile under DOS. The program is called **depends** and we describe it in Chapter 5 and Appendix E.

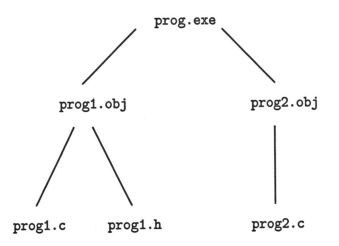

Figure 2.2: Dependency Tree

2.6 Summary

We can control the execution of the **make** command by invoking *make* with options. We can also specify a target for *make* to build. For example:

        nmake   -n

or

        nmake   -n   target

runs *make* without actually building any target. *make* lists the files that will be affected and the commands that will be executed when we run *make* without the -n flag.

        nmake -f filename

or

        nmake -f filename target

runs *make* using the set of rules in *filename* (instead of the default **makefile**). When we use the **f** option, the file name must immediately follow the flag; and Borland's *make* requires the file name to follow the flag with no spaces:

```
make -ffilename
```

The **make** command can take any number of options, and the options can appear in any order. When we invoke *make* with a target as well as options, the target must be the last item on the command line.

Each dependency item in a makefile has one or more commands associated with it. The commands can be hard-coded, or they can be written with macros. A hard-coded command appears with its target and is fixed; for example, the same compiler is used with the same compiler options every time *make* is invoked for the makefile.

Macros provide an alternative to hard-coded commands. We can define any number of macros in a makefile by assigning a value (such as a command or a text string) to each macro name. On a command line, a macro name has $( ) around it, which tells *make* to use the value assigned to the macro. Macros offer several advantages:

- The makefile is more flexible. We can use a different compiler or specify different compiler options simply by redefining a macro in one place instead of making changes throughout the makefile.

- The makefile is less likely to contain errors. We assign a value to a macro in one place; if we make a mistake, we have to correct in only one place.

A C program that appears as a dependency in a makefile may include one or more header files. A header file must be stated as a dependency along with the C program in which it is included.

Chapter 3

More About MAKE

In this chapter we continue our progress toward mastering *make*. We revisit and expand on topics introduced in the earlier chapters and introduce some new concepts that we will build on when we meet the advanced topics covered in later chapters.

For example, in Chapter 2 we began to learn about the use of macros in makefiles. We also met some of the options we can use when we invoke *make* from the command line. In this chapter, we build on that foundation, learning more about the intricacies of macros and discovering how to find out about the values of macros in our makefile by issuing an option with the **make** command.

Among the topics covered in Chapter 1 were targets and explicit commands in makefiles. In this chapter, we meet a special kind of target called a pseudotarget. In addition, we make good on our promise to tell you about inference rules and implicit commands.

Finally, this chapter offers two sample makefiles of interest. One serves as a progress check to let you see how far you've come toward mastering *make*. The second illustrates an application of *make* in a real-life project; specifically, the creation of this book.

3.1   More About Macros

We introduced macros in Chapter 2. We saw that we can include several macros in a makefile to provide flexibility and consistency and to eliminate the possibility of errors.

It is a common practice (although not required) to use capital letters for macro names. Be aware, however, that all versions of *make* are case-sensitive and see `CFLAGS` and `Cflags`, for example, as two different macro names.

Another point of style is to declare all our macros at the beginning of the makefile. This technique makes it easier to find and modify macros as the project develops.

The macros we added to our makefile in Chapter 2 are called user-defined macros; that is, they are macros we created to use in our makefile. The term *user-defined* distinguishes these macros from another type of macro — *predefined* (or built-in) macros. A predefined macro is a macro whose definition is available every time we start *make*.

Let's review our makefile from Chapter 2, then make some changes to illustrate the use of user-defined and predefined macros. Here is the makefile from Chapter 2:

```
CC      = cl
CFLAGS  = -c  -W2  -O

prog.exe:  prog1.obj  prog2.obj
        $(CC)  -o prog.exe  prog1  prog2

prog1.obj:  prog1.c
        $(CC)  $(CFLAGS)  prog1.c

prog2.obj:  prog2.c
        $(CC)  $(CFLAGS)  prog2.c
```

3.1.1   User-Defined Macros

An example of a user-defined macro is `CFLAGS`, which we used in the makefile in Chapter 2:

```
CFLAGS =  -c  -W2  -O
```

User-defined macros serve a number of purposes; for example, to select a utility (such as a C compiler) and the flags that we want to apply to that utility (as we defined `CFLAGS`).

Another common use for user-defined macros is to identify the object files we need to create to build the executable program. In our example, we want to build **prog.exe** and the object files we need are **prog1.obj**

and `prog2.obj`. To make it easy to refer to these object files, we define
a macro to be a synonym for them:

```
OBJS  =  prog1.obj  prog2.obj
```

We define another macro to identify the target we want to build:

```
TARGET  =  prog.exe
```

Using these new user-defined macros along with the macros we defined
in Chapter 2, we can change the makefile to read:

```
CC     =  cl
CFLAGS =  -c  -W2  -O
OBJS   =  prog1.obj  prog2.obj
TARGET =  prog.exe

$(TARGET):  $(OBJS)
            $(CC)  -o  $(TARGET)  $(OBJS)

prog1.obj:  prog1.c
            $(CC)  $(CFLAGS)  prog1.c

prog2.obj:  prog2.c
            $(CC)  $(CFLAGS)  prog2.c
```

3.1.2 Predefined Macros

A predefined macro is a macro that the *make* utility already knows. In
other words, it is a macro whose definition is available every time we start
make.

Predefined macros vary with the version of *make* we are using. We will
talk about some common predefined macros in this section and tell you
about the specific macros available for Microsoft's NMAKE in Chapter 5
and the UNIX version of MAKE in Chapter 7. Borland does not support
predefined macros.

Our first predefined macro is `CC`, which identifies the C compiler on our
system. However, `CC` is not defined in Borland's MAKE. In Microsoft's
NMAKE the predefined macro `CC` is equivalent to:

```
CC = cl
```

In the UNIX version of MAKE the predefined macro CC is equivalent to:

```
CC = cc
```

Well, now — here's a pleasant surprise. The CC macro is predefined; this means we do not have to explicitly define CC in our makefile (unless we are using Borland's MAKE).

Another predefined macro is $@. This macro is a synonym for the current target. In this fragment from our makefile

```
prog.exe:  prog1.obj  prog2.obj
           $(CC)  -o  prog.exe  prog1.obj  prog2.obj
```

the target is prog.exe, so the value of $@ is prog.exe. Notice that on the command line we ask CC to put the output in the file prog.exe:

```
-o  prog.exe
```

Instead of retyping the target name, we can use the predefined macro $@ because it is a synonym for the current target:

```
prog.exe:  prog1.obj  prog2.obj
           $(CC)  -o  $@  prog1.obj  prog2.obj
```

Our next predefined macro is $*. This macro is a synonym for the target name *without* an extension. Consider this fragment, for example:

```
prog1.obj:  prog1.c
            $(CC)  $(CFLAGS)  prog1.c
```

Here the target is prog1.obj. The target without an extension is prog1, so the value of $* is prog1. Using this predefined macro we can change the command line to read

```
$(CC)  $(CFLAGS)  $*.c
```

which still means 'apply the value of CC with CFLAGS to prog1.c.'

If we use the user-defined macro CFLAGS (from Chapter 2) and the three predefined macros CC, $@, and $*, our makefile becomes:

```
CFLAGS  =  -c -W2  -O

prog.exe:  prog1.obj  prog2.obj
           $(CC)  -o  $@  prog1.obj  prog2.obj
```

```
prog1.obj:  prog1.c
         $(CC)  $(CFLAGS)  $*.c

prog2.obj:  prog2.c
         $(CC)  $(CFLAGS)  $*.c
```

Notice that we have removed the macro definition

```
CC = cl
```

from the makefile because it is a predefined macro for the version of *make* we are using. (However, if we were using Borland's *make*, we would keep the definition in the makefile.) On the first command line, we have replaced the target file name **prog.exe** with **$@**; and on the other command lines we have replaced the source file names **prog1.c** and **prog2.c** with **$*.c**. The macro **$@** takes the value of the current target; and the macro **$*** takes the value of the current target without an extension.

Now let's add the macros we defined at the beginning of this chapter. We can see that our makefile has changed considerably from where we started:

```
CFLAGS =  -c  -W2  -O
OBJS   =  prog1.obj  prog2.obj
TARGET =  prog.exe

$(TARGET):  $(OBJS)
         $(CC)  -o  $@  $(OBJS)

prog1.obj:  prog1.c
         $(CC)  $(CFLAGS)  $*.c

prog2.obj:  prog2.c
         $(CC)  $(CFLAGS)  $*.c
```

In this example, the user-defined macro TARGET expands to **prog.exe**, so the value of the predefined macro **$@** is **prog.exe**.

Another useful predefined macro is **$<**, which is a synonym for the dependent file. We discuss **$<** in Section 3.3.

3.1.3   Macros and the p Option

Sometimes we need to find out the values of macros that we are using in a makefile. We may want to check the default values that *make* is using, or we think the default values are not what we want to use. An easy way to get this information is to invoke **nmake** with the **n** option and the **p** option:

```
nmake  -n  -p
```

Recall from Chapter 2 that the **n** option tells *make* to check what it should execute in a makefile without actually executing anything. The **p** option tells *make* to display the macro information. This is an easy way to find out the values of the macros *make* is using in the makefile.

3.2   Pseudotargets

Pseudotargets look like targets. However, unlike true targets, they are not files. A pseudotarget can be user-defined or predefined.

3.2.1   User-Defined Pseudotargets

User-defined pseudotargets normally appear toward the end of the makefile.

A user-defined pseudotarget is a place holder for one or more commands. Occasionally we need to execute those commands so we create a pseudotarget and list the commands after it. For example, in these lines

```
cleanup:
        erase *.obj      # erase object files
        erase *.exe      # erase executable files
```

cleanup is a user-defined pseudotarget. Two **erase** commands are associated with it. When we issue

```
nmake  cleanup
```

on the command line, *make* executes the commands following the pseudotarget. cleanup is not a file and it does not have dependencies (there are no file names after the colon (:)).

A pseudotarget without dependencies is always true; that is, *make* will invoke all the commands associated with the pseudotarget every time *make* either reaches the pseudotarget or is invoked with the pseudotarget.

3.2.2   Predefined Pseudotargets

Predefined pseudotargets are names that begin with a dot (.) and consist of uppercase letters. As with a 'true' target, the name of the pseudotarget is followed by a colon. For example,

    .SILENT:

is a predefined pseudotarget. (Borland's MAKE refers to pseudotargets as 'dot directives'.) Predefined pseudotargets usually appear at the beginning of the makefile.

.SILENT: tells *make* to not display lines as they are executed. This is equivalent to invoking *make* with the **s** option:

    nmake -s

Another pseudotarget is

    .IGNORE:

which tells *make* to ignore the codes returned by the commands that *make* invokes to accomplish its job. This is equivalent to using the **i** option with *make*.

Why use .IGNORE:? Regardless of the version of *make* we use, *make* abandons execution any time a command it has invoked fails. In this case, *make* receives a return code that indicates an error. Sometimes we do not want *make* to stop if an error is encountered. .IGNORE: tells *make* to ignore the return codes and to continue executing.

One more predefined pseudotarget is .SUFFIXES:. NMAKE and UNIX MAKE support .SUFFIXES: while Borland's MAKE does not. The versions of *make* that support .SUFFIXES: maintain a built-in list of extensions and inference rules. When *make* knows of an extension, *make* can search for either a built-in or a user-defined rule that defines the commands to be applied when it transforms a file with that extension.

We can add to the extensions that *make* knows. When we use .SUFFIXES: with one or more extensions, *make* adds those extensions to its internal list. For example,

    .SUFFIXES: .inc .tex

adds the file extensions .inc and .tex to the list of extensions that *make* already knows how to handle.

When *make* finds a target without dependencies, *make* searches for a file with the same name as the target that has an extension from the list of known extensions. For example,

```
.SUFFIXES:  .inc  .tex

    ⋮

xyz.obj:
        command
```

tells *make* to search for `xyz` with one of the known extensions (like `.c`). If the search fails, *make* looks for `xyz.inc`; if *make* finds it, that is the file that *make* will use. If `xyz.inc` does not exist, *make* searches for `xyz.tex`.

Sometimes we may choose to tell *make* to ignore its built-in list. To do this, we use `.SUFFIXES:` without any file extension following it. If we then use another `.SUFFIXES:` with extensions, we guarantee that *make* knows only those extensions. For example,

```
.SUFFIXES:
.SUFFIXES:  .inc  .tex
```

first clears the list of file extensions that *make* knows, then adds `.inc` and `.tex` to the empty list.

3.3   Inference Rules and Implicit Commands

An inference rule provides *make* with a general rule that it can use to build a target with a given extension from a dependency with a given extension. Because the rule applies to the extension of a file name, it eliminates the need to repeat a given command in a makefile. Note that a file extension also is called a suffix; for this reason, you may hear inference rules referred to as suffix rules.

In our example makefile, we've seen several file name extensions (or suffixes): `exe`, `obj`, `c`. Just as with an extension to a file name, each extension in an inference rule is preceded by a period. Thus, an inference rule always begins with a period (.), which is followed by an extension, then another period, and finally another extension. For example,

```
.c.obj:
        $(CC)  $(CFLAGS)  $*.c
```

is an inference rule. This rule starts with .c.obj (that is, the two extensions: c and obj). The rule indicates that we can have a .c file as our source and can generate a .obj file from it. The command line

```
$(CC)  $(CFLAGS)  $*.c
```

indicates how *make* will accomplish that:

- use the value of CC to invoke the C compiler with the flags specified in CFLAGS

- use the current target without an extension ($*)

- add the extension (suffix) c to $* to build the file name that CC should compile

An inference rule, then, consists of an implicit target, an implicit dependency, and one or more implicit commands. In this case, the implicit target is the .obj file to be generated; the implicit dependency is the .c file to be compiled to create the target; and the implicit command is:

```
$(CC)  $(CFLAGS)  $*.c
```

When a makefile contains a target and a list of dependencies without an explicit command line, *make* searches for an inference rule it can apply. When it finds the applicable inference rule, *make* executes the implicit commands. The commands are implicit — as contrasted with the explicit commands we talked about in Chapter 1 — because they do not appear explicitly with the target and dependencies to which they are applied.

It is time to discuss another predefined macro: $<. This macro is a synonym for the dependent file that is out-of-date with respect to the target. For example, in the inference rule we discussed earlier,

```
.c.obj:
        $(CC)  $(CFLAGS)  $*.c
```

$* is the current target without an extension. $*.c is then the name of the file to be compiled. Because $< is a synonym for the dependent file in inference rules, we can use

```
.c.obj:
        $(CC)  $(CFLAGS)  $<
```

to convey the same information as the earlier rule.

Most versions of *make* allow $< to appear only in inference rules. Borland's MAKE does not restrict the use of $<. In fact, Borland's MAKE does not have the predefined macro $@. Consequently, in Borland we use $< in place of $@:

```
prog.exe:  prog1.obj  prog2.obj
        $(CC)  -e$<  prog1.obj  prog2.obj
```

In this case $< is a synonym for the target.

In the next section, we will see some examples of how to use inference rules and implicit commands.

As with macros, there are two types of inference rules: user-defined and predefined. We will use our makefile from Chapter 2 to show how both types of inference rules are used.

3.3.1   User-Defined Inference Rules

We learned earlier in this chapter that CC is a predefined macro for our version of *make* so we have removed its definition from the makefile. With that change, here is the makefile from Chapter 2 again:

```
CFLAGS =  -c  -W2  -O
OBJS   =  prog1.obj  prog2.obj
TARGET =  prog.exe

$(TARGET):  $(OBJS)
        $(CC)  -o  $@  $(OBJS)

prog1.obj:  prog1.c
        $(CC)  $(CFLAGS)  $*.c

prog2.obj:  prog2.c
        $(CC)  $(CFLAGS)  $*.c
```

We have four macros: the predefined CC and the user-defined macros CFLAGS, OBJS, and TARGET. Every time we invoke the compiler, we use these macros. The macro mechanism provides uniformity in the makefile. For example, we initialize CFLAGS in one place, then use the value of CFLAGS — $(CFLAGS) — wherever we refer to the C compiler. But we still explicitly invoke the compiler when we want to convert a .c file into a .obj file:

```
prog1.obj:  prog1.c
        $(CC)  $(CFLAGS)  prog1.c
```

As we said earlier, the inference rule provides a general rule for creating a new file from an existing file. Recall, for example, that to convert a .c file into a .obj file we use the inference rule:

```
.c.obj:
        $(CC)  $(CFLAGS)  $*.c
```

This is an inference rule we created for *make* to use when it determines that a .c file needs to be compiled (in effect, *make* generates a .obj file from a .c file).

Remember that when the makefile has a target and a list of dependencies without an explicit command line, *make* searches for an inference rule that it can apply. For example, using the inference rule

```
.c.obj:
        $(CC)  $(CFLAGS)  $*.c
```

and the target/dependency line

```
prog1.obj:  prog1.c
```

make applies the command line

```
$(CC)  $(CFLAGS)  $*.c
```

to build prog1.obj from prog1.c. Remember we defined

```
CFLAGS  =  -c  -W2  -O
```

CC is predefined

```
CC  =  cl
```

and $* is predefined to be the name of the current target without an extension. Then *make* understands that the command line, in this case, is:

```
cl  -c  -W2  -O  prog1.c
```

Using macros and an inference rule, the makefile becomes:

```
CFLAGS  =  -c  -W2  -O

.c.obj:
        $(CC)  $(CFLAGS)  $*.c

prog.exe:   prog1.obj  prog2.obj
        $(CC)  -o  prog.exe  prog1.obj  prog2.obj

prog1.obj:  prog1.c

prog2.obj:  prog2.c
```

Notice that the command lines are not present after the targets `prog1.obj` and `prog2.obj`; that is, these targets do not have any explicit commands associated with them. *make* knows *implicitly* how to build `prog1.obj` from `prog1.c` and `prog2.obj` from `prog2.c` by applying the command line from the inference rule `.c.obj`.

We can use the predefined macro `$@`, define our own macros `TARGET` and `OBJS` (as we did earlier in this chapter), and construct a new makefile that is easier to maintain:

```
CFLAGS  =  -c  -W2  -O
OBJS    =  prog1.obj  prog2.obj
TARGET  =  prog.exe

.c.obj:
        $(CC)  $(CFLAGS)  $*.c

$(TARGET):  $(OBJS)
        $(CC)  -o  $@  $(OBJS)
```

We do not need to include the targets `prog1.obj:` and `prog2.obj:` because *make* knows how to find the dependencies based on the inference rules.

We can use any number of commands in an inference rule. In this example, one command was sufficient. We can create inference rules for any conversion we find necessary in our makefile. For example, when we deal with assembly language we define the macros

```
AS     =  masm
AFLAGS =
```

because we want to use Microsoft's masm assembler without any flags. The inference rule we want to use in this case is:

```
.asm.obj:
        $(AS)  $(AFLAGS)  $*.asm
```

Why have we defined AFLAGS to be empty? Simply put, at this time we do not need any options. AFLAGS is present as a place holder. When we decide we need one or more options to apply to the assembler, we change AFLAGS without disturbing the rest of the makefile.

The technique of defining an empty macro is an example of planning ahead in a development project. A more experienced software developer might define an empty macro almost without thinking about it, while a less experienced programmer might completely overlook the usefulness of such a place holder. If you forget about it, don't be discouraged. Even the most experienced programmers revise their makefiles many times as a project evolves.

3.3.2 Predefined Inference Rules

Most versions of *make* know about common file extensions, such as .c and .obj. This means that, in many instances, *make* already has a predefined rule for obtaining a .obj file from a .c file. (Note, however, that Borland does not support predefined inference rules.)

For example, the NMAKE command from Microsoft uses the predefined rule

```
.c.obj:
        $(CC)  $(CFLAGS)  -c  $*.c
```

where the macros CC and CFLAGS are preset to:

```
CC     =  cl
CFLAGS =
```

As we saw in the previous section, a macro can be empty. Here, CFLAGS is an empty macro.

Defining our own macros and using the predefined inference rules of NMAKE, we can change our makefile to read:

```
TARGET =  prog.exe
CFLAGS =  -W2  -O
OBJS   =  prog1.obj  prog2.obj

$(TARGET):  $(OBJS)
          $(CC)  -o  $@  $(OBJS)
```

Notice that the built-in list of extensions maintained by .SUFFIXES: and the predefined inference rules allow us to eliminate the dependency lines for prog1.obj and prog2.obj. Remember that if we are using Borland's MAKE, the makefile must contain the inference rule because the are no predefined inference rules.

For another example, let's modify our makefile to run on a UNIX system. Before we do, there are some things we need to know about files in UNIX systems. For example, in UNIX systems (as in DOS) the extension for a C file is .c. However, the extension for an object file in UNIX systems is .o (unlike DOS, where it is .obj). Because the *make* command in UNIX systems already knows about these extensions, it uses the predefined inference rule

```
.c.o:
          $(CC)  -c  $(CFLAGS)  $*.c
```

where the macros CC and CFLAGS are preset to:

```
CC     =  cc
CFLAGS =  -O
```

Here's something else we should know about UNIX files: executable files are not required to have special extensions like .exe or .com. So we'll call our executable file prog.

We do not need to define an inference rule to produce a .o file from a .c file because that inference rule is predefined. Nor do we need to initialize the CC and CFLAGS macros because their predefined values are acceptable for our purposes.

The makefile then becomes:

```
TARGET =  prog
OBJS   =  prog1.o  prog2.o

$(TARGET):  $(OBJS)
          $(CC)  -o  $@  $(OBJS)
```

Your version of *make* may support other inference rules. Remember, too, that invoking *make* with the p option displays all predefined values, including predefined inference rules.

3.4 How Are We Doing?

Let's stop here and see how much we've learned about makefiles. By now, you should be able to read a makefile and understand its elements, the relationships between them, and the functions the makefile performs.

The next example will give you a chance to test yourself on what you've learned. But before we show you the example, let's talk about what we mean by being able to read and understand a makefile.

The purpose of this book is to guide you through the process of creating a makefile that you can apply to a particular program development project. It is not our purpose to teach you about your compiler. So that when you see a macro definition like

```
CFLAGS =  -c  -W2  -O
```

and a command line that includes macros like

```
$(CC)  $(CFLAGS)  prog1.c
```

you should understand that *make* expands the macro $(CFLAGS) to its value -c -W2 -O. If you know, for example, that -W2 is a compiler option that means 'set warnings to level 2', you're in great shape! But if you don't know that fact, it doesn't mean you don't understand makefiles; rather, it means you need to refer to your compiler documentation to find out more about compiler options.

Here is an example makefile for you to test yourself on. If you can read it and understand what *make* will do as it executes the makefile, you are ready to move on to the advanced topics in the next chapter. If you aren't completely sure of your understanding of this example, you should review the information we have presented up to now.

```
.SUFFIXES:
.SUFFIXES:  .c  .asm  .obj  .exe

# Define Macros
```

```
TARGET  =  sample
AFLAGS  =
CFLAGS  =  -c  -W2  -O
OBJS    =  sample1.obj  sample2.obj

# Define Inference Rules

.asm.obj:
        $(AS)  $(AFLAGS)  $*.asm ;

.c.obj:
        $(CC)  $(CFLAGS)  $*.c

# Define Target

$(TARGET).exe: $(OBJS)
        $(CC)  -o  $@  $(OBJS)
        copy  $@  a:$@
        attrib +r  a:$@

# List Indirect Dependencies

sample1.obj:    sample1.c               \
                sample1.h

sample2.obj:    sample2.asm             \
                sample.inc
```

Here are some hints:

- See Section 3.2 for information about .SUFFIXES:.

- See Section 1.2.1 for the use of #.

- See Section 3.1 for a discussion of user-defined and predefined macros.

- See Section 3.3 for information about inference rules.

- See Section 1.2.1 for the use of \.

3.5   Application: Makefile for Text Formatting

So far our makefiles have dealt with compilations and links. However, we can apply *make* to other tasks.

For example, we used *make* to assemble this book. We began by creating one file per chapter. Each chapter has a .inc extension, so our chapter files are named ch1.inc, ch2.inc, etc.

In addition to creating the text chapters, we wrote a program, which we called include. This program copies (includes) examples from our system directly into the text of the chapter. The text for a chapter plus the included examples form a .tex file. The final product is a device-independent file with the extension .dvi.

Before we get into the makefile we created to accomplish the task of assembling the book, let's talk about some terms you'll see:

- TEXFILES is a macro we defined in the makefile to represent all the chapters with examples included.

- book.tex is a small file that refers to the individual chapters and appendices that make up the book.

- latex is a command that invokes the collection of macros that our text formatting program uses to format our files.

In brief, when latex is invoked it produces the .dvi file from book.tex and TEXFILES. Now for the details.

We started our makefile by asking *make* to forget any knowledge of predefined inference rules and suffixes

```
.SUFFIXES:
```

then stated which suffixes are valid for this makefile:

```
.SUFFIXES:        .inc .tex .dvi
```

The inference rule we defined for generating a .tex file from a .inc file is:

```
.inc.tex:
        include <$*.inc >$*.tex
```

In other words, a `.inc` file provides the input to the program **include**, which writes its output to a `.tex` file. Thus, for example, when *make* encounters **ch1.tex** in the makefile as it executes, it looks for **ch1.inc** and directs the contents of that file to the program **include**, which in turn creates the file **ch1.tex**.

The target **book.dvi** depends on TEXFILES and **book.tex**:

```
book.dvi:        $(TEXFILES)  book.tex
        latex  book.tex
```

Here is the complete makefile:

```
.SUFFIXES:
.SUFFIXES:        .inc .tex .dvi

TEXFILES=         pre.tex         \
                  ch1.tex         \
                  ch2.tex         \
                  ch3.tex         \
                  ch4.tex         \
                  ch5.tex         \
                  ch6.tex         \
                  ch7.tex         \
                  apa.tex         \
                  apb.tex         \
                  apc.tex         \
                  apd.tex         \
                  ape.tex

.inc.tex:
        include  <$*.inc  >$*.tex

book.dvi:        $(TEXFILES)  book.tex
        latex  book.tex
```

3.6   Summary

We can use two types of macros in a makefile: user-defined and predefined. As a matter of convention, we capitalize the names of user-defined macros and place them at the beginning of the makefile.

We use $( ) around the macro name when we want *make* to use
the value assigned to the macro. When the macro name consists of one
character (such as some of the predefined macros), the parentheses are
not required. For example, we use $(CC) (more than one character), but
$* (one character).

A special type of user-defined macro is an empty macro, which we
create to serve as a place holder for future use as the project develops.

We can find out the names and default values of predefined and user-
defined macros, as well as inference rules and pseudotargets, by invoking
make on the command line with the p option and the n option:

```
nmake  -p  -n
```

If necessary, we can change the value of any predefined macro by
assigning it a new value in the same way that we assign a value to a user-
defined macro. By convention, we place redefined macros (along with
user-defined macros) at the beginning of the makefile.

Some predefined macros are:

- CC = cl (for NMAKE)

- CC = cc (for the UNIX version of MAKE)

- CC is not defined for MAKE from Borland

- $@ = the current target (including the extension, if any; not defined
  for Borland)

- $* = the current target without an extension (the base file name)

- $< = a dependent file out-of-date with the target file (in Borland,
  replaces $@)

A pseudotarget is, as the name implies, not a true target. No file
is associated with the target name, and no dependencies follow the
target name in the makefile. As with macros, there are two varieties
of pseudotargets: user-defined and predefined.

User-defined pseudotargets conventionally appear toward the end
of the makefile (in contrast to user-defined macros). The commands
associated with the pseudotarget are always executed, either when *make*
reaches the pseudotarget in the makefile or when *make* is invoked with

the pseudotarget on the command line (similar to invoking *make* with the name of a 'true' target as we did in Chapter 1).

Predefined pseudotargets begin with a dot (and, for that reason, are referred to as 'dot directives' in Borland) and end with a colon. The names of predefined pseudotargets are capitalized. Some predefined pseudotargets are:

.SILENT: do not display command lines from the makefile as they are executed. Equivalent to invoking *make* with the **s** option.

.IGNORE: ignore codes returned by commands that *make* invokes as it executes. Equivalent to invoking *make* with the **i** option.

.SUFFIXES: maintains a built-in list of file extensions that *make* uses to build a target that does not have any dependencies. (Borland does not support this pseudotarget.)

A useful application of the .SUFFIXES: pseudotarget is to create a list of project-specific suffixes (or file extensions) after first telling *make* to forget the suffixes it already knows about; for example:

```
.SUFFIXES:
.SUFFIXES:  .inc  .tex  .dvi
```

An inference rule (also called a suffix rule) consists of an implicit target, an implicit dependency, and one or more implicit commands. *make* uses inference rules to determine what action to take when it finds a target/dependency line in a makefile without any explicit commands.

The first line of an inference rule contains the extension of a source file (which provides the implicit dependency) followed by the extension of a file to be built (which is the implicit target). A dot precedes each extension, and the line ends with a colon. The implicit commands associated with the inference rule begin on the next line and adhere to the same rules of indentation as explicit commands (refer to Chapter 1).

All versions of *make* support user-defined inference rules. NMAKE from Microsoft and MAKE in UNIX systems support predefined inference rules; Borland's MAKE does not.

A predefined inference rule for NMAKE from Microsoft is:

```
.c.obj:
        $(CC)  $(CFLAGS)  -c  $*.c
```

A predefined inference rule for MAKE in UNIX systems is:

```
.c.o:
        $(CC)  $(CFLAGS)  -c  $<
```

Chapters 5 and 7 list more inference rules for these two versions of *make*.

Chapter 4

Advanced Topics

As we've seen, *make* is a powerful tool that can perform a wide variety of the tasks associated with managing software development. We've learned that by using macros, pseudotargets, and inference rules we can expand the usefulness of our makefile and, thus, the power of *make*.

We're ready now to begin investigating more advanced ways we can use *make*. Recursion, environment variables, and input files are techniques available with all versions of *make*. In-line response is available to DOS versions of *make*. We'll see in this chapter how to take advantage of these powerful devices. Advanced techniques that apply only to one or another specific version of *make* are covered, as appropriate, in the concluding chapters.

4.1 Using MAKE Recursively

We can get *make* to do more work for us by using *make* recursively. To put it another way, we can apply the property of recursion to *make*. What does this mean? What is recursion?

In simple terms, for our case recursion means that *make* can re-execute itself, if necessary, and possibly use different makefiles in the process. Let's look briefly at a small example that will help clear up this matter of recursion.

Suppose we have a directory called `top`. Below this directory are three directories called `middle1`, `middle2`, and `middle3`. The tree would look like this:

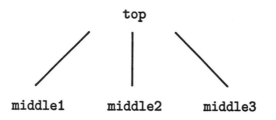

Figure 4.1: Directory Structure

Now, with this structure in mind, let's say each of the middle directories contains source code files and a makefile. We want to create a makefile in top that will invoke *make* in each of the three subdirectories.

What would that makefile look like? Here is an example of a makefile to perform that very task:

```
all:
        cd  middle1
        $(MAKE)
        cd  ..\middle2
        $(MAKE)
        cd  ..\middle3
        $(MAKE)
        cd  ..
```

The last command (cd ..) brings us back to the parent directory of middle3; that is, it brings us back to the directory where *make* started executing commands. (Note that the above sequence of commands in UNIX systems will not behave the same way as it does in DOS. For a UNIX example see the makefile on page 50 and an explanation in Section 7.3.)

MAKE is a predefined macro that invokes the current *make* command. In NMAKE the macro is preset to:

```
MAKE  =  nmake
```

This makefile certainly looks very different from the ones we've seen in earlier chapters. Let's look more closely at this makefile.

The first thing we notice is that this makefile has *no* dependencies, and, in place of the usual target, we are using a pseudotarget called **all**. We met pseudotargets in Chapter 3 (page 26). Because the pseudotarget **all** has no dependencies, the original instance of *make* issues all the commands that follow the pseudotarget.

Notice that this makefile invokes *make* three separate times, once for each of the subdirectories. This gives us a clear picture of how recursion works. We invoked the first instance of *make* from the command line; then *make* invokes itself (the recursion process) by executing the command lines contained in the first makefile.

We have assumed in our example that each of the subdirectories contains a makefile; specifically, one with the default file name *make* searches for. If our assumption is wrong — if any of the subdirectories lacks this makefile — *make* will display an error message informing us of the problem.

Let's change our example so the makefile works with MAKE from Borland:

```
MAKE    =  make

all:
        cd  middle1
        $(MAKE)
        cd  ..\middle2
        $(MAKE)
        cd  ..\middle3
        $(MAKE)
        cd  ..
```

Notice that the only change is the addition of the macro **MAKE**. We must define this macro because MAKE from Borland does not assign any macros.

In our first example of using *make* recursively, the makefile expected a separate makefile each time the **make** command was issued. Another way to apply recursion is to use the same makefile for each instance of *make*. For example, we may need to re-invoke *make* within our makefile and have it use the same makefile, but with a different target. Here's a makefile that shows this recursive use of *make*:

```
# Recursion using the same makefile (Microsoft)

.SUFFIXES:
.SUFFIXES: .c .obj .exe

# Define Macros

EXEC_NAME       =  prog
CFLAGS          =  -c  -W2  -O
OBJS            =  prog1.obj  prog2.obj
MID_DIR         =  middle1

# Define target and dependencies

$(EXEC_NAME).exe:  $(OBJS) $(MID_DIR)\prog3.obj
        $(CC) -o $@ $(OBJS) $(MID_DIR)\prog3.obj

$(MID_DIR)\prog3.obj:  $(MID_DIR)\prog3.c
        cd  $(MID_DIR)
        $(MAKE)  -f ..\makefile                        \
                COMM="Compiling PROG3.C"  prog3.obj
        cd ..

prog3.obj:        prog3.c
        echo  $(COMM)
        $(CC) $(CFLAGS) prog3.c
```

Notice that we have added a new direct dependency to **prog.exe**. It is an object file called **prog3.obj**. Before **prog3.obj** can be created, we must change directories to **middle1** and, while in that subdirectory, we re-invoke *make* to execute the makefile in the parent directory; that is, the same makefile currently being executed by the first instance of *make*.

Let's look again at a couple of sections of our makefile. The section where *make* is re-invoked

```
$(MID_DIR)\prog3.obj:  $(MID_DIR)\prog3.c
        cd  $(MID_DIR)
        $(MAKE)  -f ..\makefile                        \
                COMM="Compiling PROG3.C"  prog3.obj
        cd ..
```

and the indirect dependency line for `prog3.obj`:

```
prog3.obj:      prog3.c
        echo  $(COMM)
        $(CC) $(CFLAGS) prog3.c
```

Notice how we have used the macro we named MID_DIR as a path to the files `prog3.obj` and `prog3.c`. We use this technique because the initial instance of make is running from `top`, the parent directory, so we have to tell *make* where to find `prog3.*`.

On the other hand, we do *not* use the MID_DIR macro in the indirect dependency statement for `prog3.obj`. The macro is not required here because *make* has already issued the command

```
cd  $(MID_DIR)
```

so that the current directory is `middle1`, where all the `prog3` files reside.

Returning to the line that re-invokes *make*, we see two other points of interest: we have specified a target, `prog3.obj`; and we have defined a new macro that is passed to the second invocation of *make*. When this second instance of *make* executes the command line

```
echo  $(COMM)
```

it expands the macro COMM to display the message

```
Compiling PROG3.C
```

before compiling the program. When the second instance of *make* has finished creating `prog3.obj`, it returns to the original process and the initial instance of *make* continues to create the target, `prog.exe`.

One question we might ask is: Why put all the dependencies for the `middle1` program into the `top` makefile? The reason is simple. It requires only a small amount of work to build `prog3.obj`, so we can use the existing makefile to perform all that is needed. A second reason is we do not want to maintain duplicate copies of a makefile to produce the same results.

Now let's look at the same makefile for MAKE from Borland:

```
# Recursion using the same makefile (Borland)

# Define Macros

EXEC_NAME      =  prog
CC             =  tcc
CFLAGS         =  -c  -O
OBJS           =  prog1.obj    prog2.obj
MID_DIR        =  middle1
MAKE           =  make


# Define inference rule

.c.obj:
     $(CC)  $(CFLAGS)  $*.c


# Define target and dependencies

$(EXEC_NAME).exe:  $(OBJS) $(MID_DIR)\prog3.obj
       $(CC) -e$< $(OBJS) $(MID_DIR)\prog3.obj

$(MID_DIR)\prog3.obj:  $(MID_DIR)\prog3.c
       cd  $(MID_DIR)
       $(MAKE) -f..\makefile                          \
            -DCOMM=PROG3.C prog3.obj
       cd ..

prog3.obj:       prog3.c
       echo  $(COMM)
       $(CC) $(CFLAGS) prog3.c
```

We've made a few subtle changes to the makefile. First, we defined the macro CC to have the value tcc because Borland's MAKE does not have predefined macros. Second, we defined a macro called MAKE. The third change is the command line

```
$(CC) -e$< $(OBJS) $(MID_DIR)\prog3.obj
```

that produces the target prog.exe.

The fourth change is the omission of .SUFFIXES: because Borland's MAKE does not support that predefined pseudotarget.

The final change is the way we invoke Borland's MAKE with a macro defined on the command line:

```
$(MAKE) -f..\makefile                    \
        -DCOMM=PROG3.C prog3.obj
```

We tell MAKE that we are defining a macro on the command line by using the D option. Borland's MAKE also imposes a limitation on the definition of the macro: the string that follows the equal sign (=) cannot contain spaces, tabs, or quotation marks.

As we've just seen, the makefile for Microsoft's NMAKE and the makefile for Borland's MAKE are basically the same. The changes we've made in the makefile for Borland's MAKE have to do with:

- macros that were not predefined (CC and MAKE)

- a different compiler option (-e as opposed to -o)

- a different predefined macro ($< as opposed to $@)

- a different method of passing a macro from the command line to *make*

- a predefined pseudotarget (.SUFFIXES: is not supported)

Finally, let's look at the UNIX version of this makefile.

```
# Recursion using the same makefile (UNIX Systems)

.SUFFIXES:
.SUFFIXES:         .c  .o

# Define Macros

EXEC_NAME        =  prog
OBJS             =  prog1.o  prog2.o
MID_DIR          =  middle1

# Define target and dependencies

$(EXEC_NAME):    $(OBJS) $(MID_DIR)/prog3.o
        $(CC) -o $@ $(OBJS) $(MID_DIR)/prog3.o

$(MID_DIR)/prog3.o:  $(MID_DIR)/prog3.c
        cd  $(MID_DIR) ;                              \
        $(MAKE)  -f  ../makefile                      \
                COMM="Compiling PROG3.C" prog3.o

prog3.o:          prog3.c
        echo  $(COMM)
        $(CC) $(CFLAGS) -c prog3.c
```

A quick comparison reveals that only a few changes were needed to convert the makefile from use with Microsoft's NMAKE for use on UNIX systems. Here is what we did:

- Removed the .exe extension

- Treated cd $(MID_DIR) and the act of re-invoking *make* as one process (see Chapter 7)

- Changed the object file extensions from .obj to .o

- Changed the backslashes (\) in directory paths to forward slashes (/)

The rest of the makefile is untouched.

When we look at these three makefiles side by side, we see that they are essentially the same. We may need to make a few, relatively simple changes to adapt a makefile that works for one version of *make* for use with another version, thus highlighting one of the valuable features of *make*.

4.2   Using Environment Variables in Makefiles

Makefiles can access and use environment variables. But just what is an environment variable? We know that a variable is a name to which a value is assigned and that the assigned value can be changed at will as needed. The environment is the collection of definitions required by the operating system to perform basic tasks, such as displaying a prompt and searching directories for command files.

Thus, an environment variable is a variable that is defined in and controls some aspect of the system's environment. This means that each program that runs on the system is aware of and can use the environment information that the variable provides.

To determine what your system's environment consists of, enter **set** at the command line. The **set** command displays all the environment variables known to your system. For example, the following is a list of known variables we might see if we entered **set** on a DOS machine:

```
COMSPEC=c:\command.com
PATH=C:\;C:\DOS
```

In UNIX systems you can use **set** or **env** to check the system's environment. The reference manual for your operating system discusses the environment variables it uses.

To create a new variable in the environment, we simply enter the **set** command followed by the variable name and the value we want to assign to it in the form:

```
set VARIABLE_NAME=VALUE
```

Sometimes we want to change the value of an environment variable the system already knows about, such as PATH. Sometimes we want to create a brand-new environment variable because we use a program that expects to find such an environment variable. For example, the environment does not know about ROOTDIR, but a program could look for ROOTDIR and take the appropriate actions when it finds it. Before we use such a program, we must create a new environment variable, ROOTDIR.

In terms of using environment variables in makefiles, an environment variable can be used very much like a macro. To illustrate, for our DOS example let's create an environment variable called ROOTDIR that we can use in our makefile. We create the variable by entering at the command line:

```
set ROOTDIR=\root
```

If we look at the DOS environment list again (using **set**), we see the following:

```
COMSPEC=c:\command.com
PATH=C:\;C:\DOS
ROOTDIR=\root
```

Now that we have set a new environment variable, let's look at a makefile that uses the variable:

```
# Using environment variables (Microsoft)

.SUFFIXES:
.SUFFIXES: .c .obj .exe

# Define Macros

EXEC_NAME     = prog
CFLAGS        = -c  -W2  -O
OBJS          = prog1.obj  prog2.obj
MID_DIR       = middle1

# Define target and dependencies

$(ROOTDIR)\$(EXEC_NAME).exe:  $(ROOTDIR)\$(OBJS)    \
                     $(MID_DIR)\prog3.obj
        cd  $(ROOTDIR)
        $(CC) -o $@ $(OBJS) $(MID_DIR)\prog3.obj

$(MID_DIR)\prog3.obj:  $(MID_DIR)\prog3.c
        cd  $(MID_DIR)
```

```
        $(MAKE) -f $(ROOTDIR)\makefile              \
               COMM="Compiling PROG3.C"  prog3.obj
        cd  $(ROOTDIR)

# Define indirect dependencies

$(ROOTDIR)\prog1.obj:   prog1.c

$(ROOTDIR)\prog2.obj:   prog2.c

prog3.obj:              prog3.c
        echo  $(COMM)
        $(CC) $(CFLAGS) prog3.c
```

We've changed our earlier makefile in several places by using the environment variable ROOTDIR. Because *make* automatically includes all environment variables during execution, they can be referred to as if they were macros. Notice that the target in this makefile is stated as

```
$(ROOTDIR)\$(EXEC_NAME).exe
```

which uses the environment variable ROOTDIR as a macro in the same manner as the user-defined macro EXEC_NAME.

The changes we've made to the makefile allow *make* to be used from anywhere in the system; we are no longer limited to issuing **make** from a single directory. By using an environment variable in our makefile, we've added again to the flexibility and power of *make*.

Let's look at this makefile modified for the MAKE command from Borland:

```
# Using environment variables (Borland)

# Define Macros

EXEC_NAME       = prog
CC              = tcc
CFLAGS          = -c  -O
OBJS            = prog1.obj  prog2.obj
MID_DIR         = middle1
MAKE            = make


# Define inference rules

.c.obj:
        $(CC)  $(CFLAGS)  $*.c

# Define target and dependencies

$(ROOTDIR)\$(EXEC_NAME).exe:  $(ROOTDIR)\$(OBJS)      \
                $(MID_DIR)\prog3.obj
        cd  $(ROOTDIR)
        $(CC) -e$< $(OBJS) $(MID_DIR)\prog3.obj


$(MID_DIR)\prog3.obj:  $(MID_DIR)\prog3.c
        cd  $(MID_DIR)
        $(MAKE)  -f$(ROOTDIR)\makefile                \
                -DCOMM=PROG3.C prog3.obj
        cd  $(ROOTDIR)

# Define indirect dependencies

$(ROOTDIR)\prog1.obj:   prog1.c

$(ROOTDIR)\prog2.obj:   prog2.c

prog3.obj:              prog3.c
        echo  $(COMM)
        $(CC) $(CFLAGS) prog3.c
```

As with the earlier examples, only minor changes have been made to adapt the makefile for use with Borland's MAKE. These changes are new values for the CC, CFLAGS, and COMM macros and the creation of the MAKE macro. The $(CC) command line is also different to accommodate the use of the tcc command (we use -e$< instead of -o $@).

Here is the modified makefile for use on UNIX systems:

```
# Using environment variables (UNIX Systems)

.SUFFIXES:
.SUFFIXES: .c .o

# Define Macros

EXEC_NAME       =   prog
OBJS            =   prog1.o  prog2.o
MID_DIR         =   middle1

# Define target and dependencies

$(ROOTDIR)/$(EXEC_NAME):        $(ROOTDIR)/$(OBJS)  \
            $(MID_DIR)/prog3.o
        cd  $(ROOTDIR) ;                            \
        $(CC) -o $@ $(OBJS) $(MID_DIR)/prog3.o

$(MID_DIR)/prog3.o:             $(MID_DIR)/prog3.c
        cd  $(MID_DIR) ;                            \
        $(MAKE)  -f $(ROOTDIR)/makefile             \
            COMM="Compiling PROG3.C" prog3.o

# Define indirect dependencies

$(ROOTDIR)/prog1.o:     prog1.c

$(ROOTDIR)/prog2.o:     prog2.c

prog3.o:                prog3.c
        echo  $(COMM)
        $(CC) $(CFLAGS) -c prog3.c
```

We see several minor changes to the makefile: the CFLAGS options have been changed to comply with the options for the compiler, .exe has been removed, .objs have been changed to .os, we treated cd $(MID_DIR) and the act of re-invoking *make* as one process (see Chapter 7), and, except for line continuation indicators, all backslashes (\) have been changed to forward slashes (/). No other changes were made to the makefile.

One final note about environment variables. Microsoft's NMAKE provides the e option, which restricts the makefile from changing the value of an environment variable during execution. This means that if the makefile included the statement

```
ROOTDIR=c:\tmp
```

and we invoked NMAKE with the e option, then the line in the makefile would *not* be executed and the value of ROOTDIR would remain \root (that is, the value we assigned using the set command).

You can find out more about how your version of *make* handles environment variables by referring to the documentation for your operating system and compiler.

4.3   DOS: Input Files and In-Line Response Files

Remember the very first makefile we looked at in Chapter 1? Here it is again:

```
prog.exe:  prog1.obj  prog2.obj
        cl  -o  prog.exe  prog1.obj  prog2.obj

prog1.obj:  prog1.c
        cl  -c  -W2  -O  prog1.c

prog2.obj:  prog2.c
        cl  -c  -W2  -O  prog2.c
```

Notice that we linked the .obj files and produced the target **prog.exe** using the command line:

```
cl  -o  prog.exe  prog1.obj  prog2.obj
```

An alternative to using cl to link is using the link command explicitly:

```
link  prog1.obj prog2.obj, prog.exe ;
```

Notice the semicolon (;) at the end of the **link** command line. The purpose of the semicolon is to instruct the linker to use default values for the link options instead of prompting the user for them. If we want to use only some (or none) of the default values, we simply include on the command line the options we want before (or instead of) the semicolon.

The following command line shows a case in which we have decided *not* to use all the default options:

```
link prog1+prog2, prog.exe, , slibce ;
```

This **link** command line includes an option that was not present in the earlier case: **slibce**, which tells the linker which library to bring in to link with our object files.

Notice that we retained the semicolon at the end of the command line. Without it, the linker might prompt for other options that we haven't specified. However, because the semicolon is present, the linker knows to use default values for the rest of the link options.

Our example **link** command line is pretty compact, but command lines can easily become quite lengthy. Command lines in makefiles can be particularly bothersome because *make* requires a backslash (\) at the end of a line to indicate that the next line is a continuation of the current line.

The solution to dealing with lengthy, unwieldy command lines in a makefile is simple. Using our example, we place the parameters to the **link** command in a file. Then, in the makefile, we tell the linker to use the file instead of depending on a list of parameters on the command line.

To get an idea of how this works, let's put our link parameters into a file called **makefile.lnk**. Here they are again:

```
prog1+prog2, prog, , slibce ;
```

We've just created an input file to the linker. (An input file is also referred as a response file or an autoresponse file.) To have the linker read the input file, we precede the name of the input file with the 'at' character (@). (Note that this use of @ is distinct from the predefined macro $@.) This character tells the linker to use the link information stored in the file and not to prompt for input. Now the **link** command line within the makefile looks like this:

```
link  @makefile.lnk
```

It's easy to see, even with our compact example, how helpful an input file can be. Its usefulness is even more evident when a large number of files and linker options must be used.

Now that we understand the basic concept of the input file to a linker, let's consider how we can make it even more useful. For example, what if we want to use a macro in an input file? We can do it: the linker is aware of environment variables.

Recall that earlier in this chapter we created an environment variable called ROOTDIR and showed how we could use it as if it were a macro. Here's an example of what our input file would look like using the environment variable as a macro:

```
prog1+prog2, $(ROOTDIR)\prog, , slibce ;
```

Closely related to input files are in-line response files. The two DOS versions of *make* that we have been discussing (NMAKE from Microsoft and MAKE from Borland) support what is called in-line response.

Let's start with an example of an in-line response for NMAKE:

```
link  @<<makefile.lnk
prog1+prog2, $(ROOTDIR)\prog, , slibce ;
<<keep
```

The in-line response file begins and ends with <<. Note that if makefile.lnk already exists, it will be overwritten with input from the in-line response.

An in-line response can have more than one line. We add lines (without using backslashes) and use the second << to indicate that we do not have more lines for the in-line response:

```
link  @<<makefile.lnk
prog1+prog2,
$(ROOTDIR)\prog, ,
slibce ;
<<keep
```

In the earlier example, we told the linker (by means of the @ character) to get its parameters from a file named makefile.lnk. However, in this example, we've inserted << between the @ character and the input to

link. This format indicates that the file will be created from the items that follow, beginning on the next line and continuing up to the next <<. A file created in this manner is called an in-line response file.

Note that a file created by in-line response is a temporary file. After executing the makefile, NMAKE removes any temporary files that were created in the process. Now, we might want to save `makefile.lnk` for some future use. If we do, we must follow the << at the end of the in-line response with the command **keep**. If we are not interested in saving the file to use again, we omit **keep**. (The default is <<nokeep, which is equivalent to <<.)

Next let's look at part of a makefile using in-line response that will work with the Borland version of MAKE:

```
tlink  @<<!
prog1+prog2,  $(ROOTDIR)\prog  cs.lib
!
```

In this example, we've instructed the `tlink` command to create a temporary file (denoted by <<!) for its information. We use the @ character as we did for the NMAKE command, but the delimiters are different: <<! marks the beginning of the in-line response and ! marks the end.

A final point for this example: we do not see the word **keep** after the closing delimiter. How then can we prevent *make* from deleting this file at the completion of the makefile? The answer is that when we invoke Borland's MAKE we must specify the K option. This option prevents all temporary files from being deleted.

You can find out more about using input files and in-line response files from sources provided with your compiler: refer to the online tutorial for NMAKE, or the *Turbo C++ User's Guide* for MAKE from Borland.

4.4 Common Errors

Errors are inevitable as we develop makefiles for the projects we manage. In this section, we try to anticipate some of the errors most commonly made. We show the messages these errors produce and explain what they mean. Ideally, by knowing what the most common errors are, we can avoid them.

Error:

`No arguments or description file.`

make cannot find a file called `makefile`. If the makefile has a name other than `makefile`, then use the **f** option and the name of the file to inform *make* of the name of the makefile.

For example, if you named the file `descript.mak` and you are using NMAKE from Microsoft, use the command line:

```
nmake  -f  descript.mak
```

If you are using Borland's MAKE, use:

```
make  -fdescript.mak
```

Error:

`Must be a separator on rules line ##.`

DOS versions of *make* expect commands to be preceded by one or more tabs or spaces. You will see this message when the command starts in column 1 of the referenced line.

In the UNIX systems we use, the command must be preceded by one or more tabs (*not* space characters).

Error:

`Don't know how to make xxxxxx.`

make does not know how to make a target or a dependency. For example, the following makefile contains one target, **yyyy**, and one command:

```
yyyy:
        echo "This is target yyyy."
```

If you invoke *make* and ask it to build target **zzzz** with the command line:

```
nmake  zzzz
```

make responds that it does not know how to make **zzzz**. This is because the target **zzzz** does not exist.

make produces this message in another context: when it cannot find a file for a dependency. For example, if the makefile contains these lines

```
prog.exe:   prog.c
       cl  prog.c
```

and `prog.c` is not in the current directory, *make* tells you it does not know how to make `prog.c`.

In the versions of *make* that support the pseudotarget `.SUFFIXES:`, make sure that your *make* knows of the suffixes you are using and that *make* has an inference rule to apply to your file. Otherwise, *make* will not know how to make **xxxxxx**. (Refer to Chapter 5 for information about `.SUFFIXES:` for NMAKE and to Chapter 7 for information about MAKE on UNIX systems. MAKE from Borland does not support `.SUFFIXES:`.)

Error:

xxxxxx is up-to-date.

make checked the date and time for the dependencies of **xxxxxx** (i.e., the target being built) and found that none of the dependencies is newer than **xxxxxx**.

If your list of dependencies is correct, this is a valid message. It means that *make* did not have anything to do.

If you changed any of the files that the target **xxxxxx** depends on, then the file you modified does not appear in the dependency list for the target **xxxxxx**.

Error:

syntax error: separator missing.

make found a situation that does not follow the standard construct for a makefile:

```
macroname  =  macrovalue

target:  dependency1  dependency2 ...
        command1

    ⋮

        commandn
```

For example, these lines in a makefile

```
!ifndef  DEBUG
echo DEBUG is not defined.
!endif


yyyy:
        echo This is yyyy.
```

will produce this syntax error message. This is because the **echo** command within the **ifndef** directive does not follow a target. Remember that commands appear after targets like **yyyy:**.

Error:

line ##: syntax error.
   Line ## contains an error. If the referenced line in your makefile looks like a blank line, then the error is caused by tab characters; *make* will produce a syntax error for lines that contain only tab characters.

Error:

syntax error: 'xxxxxxx' unexpected
   In the example below, *make* found a dependency line beginning with the target **prog.exe:**. The blank line that follows the dependency line indicates the end of the command list; in this case it was empty because of the blank line. The command line that begins with **cl** is neither a target nor a part of the earlier command list.

```
    prog.exe:   prog.c

        cl  prog.c
```

Therefore, *make* will not be able to interpet it, and the message will say that **'cl'** is unexpected.

4.5   Summary

We can extend the versatility and power of *make* by using recursion, environment variables as macros, input files, and in-line response.
   Recursion is a process in which *make* re-executes itself. We can use *make* recursively in two ways:

- use a different makefile for each instance of *make*

- use the same makefile and apply it to different targets for each instance of *make*

The predefined macro MAKE facilitates the recursive use of Microsoft's NMAKE and the UNIX version of MAKE; for Borland's MAKE we must define the macro:

```
MAKE  =  make
```

Recursion allows us to define a new macro on any of the makefile command lines and to pass it to a recursive instance of *make*. Finally, using *make* recursively relieves us of the need to maintain duplicate copies of a makefile to perform the same tasks in multiple directory locations or on multiple targets.

make automatically includes all environment variables during execution. Thus, once an environment variable has been defined, it can be used in a makefile as if the variable were a predefined macro.

We use the **set** command to display all environment variables currently known to the system. We define a new variable on the command line by assigning a value to a name in the form:

```
set VARIABLE_NAME=VALUE
```

One useful application of this technique is to set a directory path so that *make* can be used from anywhere in the system.

An input file provides input to a command; in this case, to a command within a makefile. In-line response files are closely related to input files. The difference is that we create an input file external to and independent of the makefile in which it is used. In contrast, we write an in-line response file as part of the makefile, and the file is created as *make* executes.

We use the 'at' character (@) to tell a linker to use an input file. The delimiters for in-line response are different for the two DOS versions of *make*: <<...<< for Microsoft, and <<!...! for Borland. The UNIX version does not support in-line response.

We can save a file created by in-line response, but again the device for doing so varies. Microsoft supports the **keep** command after the closing in-line response delimiter:

```
<<keep
```

Borland, on the other hand, requires us to specify the K option when we invoke MAKE.

Chapter 5

Microsoft's NMAKE

In previous chapters we looked at concepts and strategies that, for the most part, apply universally to all versions of *make*. Here we focus our attention on the *make* utility NMAKE from Microsoft.

We begin this chapter by showing how to invoke NMAKE. Then we explore topics that apply specifically to Microsoft's NMAKE. Some of these topics — options, dependencies, continuation lines, and environment variables — we met earlier. New topics introduced in this chapter are preprocessor directives and the `tools.ini` file, the second of which is unique to NMAKE.

5.1 Invoking NMAKE

Here is the format for invoking NMAKE on the command line:

```
nmake  [options]  [macro_definitions]  [targets]
```

The brackets ([ ]) around a field name indicate that the field is optional. Thus, all three fields are optional for NMAKE.

5.2 Command Line Options

NMAKE supports an extensive list of command line options. If you are familiar with other versions of *make*, some of these options may look familiar. However, a number of NMAKE options differ from those supported in other versions of *make*.

NMAKE is not case sensitive with respect to options; that is, NMAKE treats a and A as the same option. Remember that when we specify an option on the command line, we must precede the option letter with a dash (-) or a forward slash (/).

Here are the options that NMAKE supports:

a	Build all targets
c	Suppress messages
d	Display modification dates
e	Let environment variables override macro definitions
f *filename*	Specify makefile
help	Display help information
i	Ignore exit/error codes
n	Display commands but do not execute them
nologo	Suppress copyright message
p	Print values of defined macros and pseudotargets
q	Return exit code
r	Ignore **tools.ini** file
s	Suppress command display while executing
t	Change target modification dates
x *filename*	Specify destination for error messages
z	Internal to Programmer's Work Bench
?	Display short help

5.3 Preprocessing Directives

A preprocessing directive is a command or an instruction that allows us to conditionally execute other commands or to conditionally select parts of a makefile. When NMAKE reads a makefile, it processes any preprocessing directives it finds before it executes commands associated with targets.

A preprocessing directive begins with an exclamation mark (!) and must appear at the beginning of the line. That is, we must place the ! in the first column on the line. However, after the ! we can use blank spaces and/or tabs, if we wish, to enhance readability of the file.

Here are the preprocessing directives that NMAKE supports:

cmdswitches	Change options in NMAKE
error *message*	Display error message
include <filename>	Insert another file as part of this makefile; NMAKE searches for the file in the directories specified in the environment variable INCLUDE.
include "filename"	Insert another file as part of this makefile; NMAKE searches for the file in the current directory.
if *expr*	Execute statements following **if** when *expr* evaluates to nonzero
ifdef *name*	Execute statements following **ifdef** when *name* has been defined as a macro
ifndef *name*	Execute statements following **ifndef** when *name* has not been defined
else	Execute statements following **else** when *expr* in the preceding **if**, or *name* in the preceding **ifdef** or **ifndef** evaluates to zero
endif	Mark the end of an **if**, **ifdef**, or **ifndef** directive
undef *name*	Undefine *name*

To see how we can apply preprocessing directives, let's start with a makefile from Chapter 3. Here is the makefile:

```
TARGET =  prog.exe
CFLAGS =  -W2  -O
OBJS   =  prog1.obj  prog2.obj

$(TARGET):  $(OBJS)
            $(CC)  -o  $@  $(OBJS)
```

Now let's modify the makefile to use directives. Here is what we want
to achieve:

- Include another makefile (called `sample.mak`) as part of our makefile. The macros we want to use will be defined in this file.

- If the `DEBUG` macro has been defined, then add the `Zi` and `Od` options
  to CFLAGS (`Zi` indicates that source debugging is ON; `Od` tells `cl` to
  disable optimization).

Here is the makefile in its new form:

```
.SUFFIXES:
.SUFFIXES: .c .obj .exe

# Include the file sample.mak

!include  "sample.mak"

!ifdef DEBUG
CFLAGS            = $(CFLAGS)  -Zi  -Od
!endif

# Target and dependencies

$(EXEC_NAME).exe:  $(OBJS)
            $(CC) -o  $@  $(OBJS)
```

Let's look more closely at the new features of this makefile, beginning
with the `include` directive. We have used the `include` directive

```
!include  "sample.mak"
```

to tell NMAKE to read the file `sample.mak` from the current directory into the current makefile. When NMAKE begins to process the makefile, it appears as if the contents of `sample.mak` were always present. Effectively, they are: the directive brings them in. Here are the contents of `sample.mak`:

```
# Define Macros

EXEC_NAME      =  prog
CFLAGS         =  -c  -W2
OBJS           =  prog1.obj  prog2.obj
```

By using the `include` directive, we can easily create part of a makefile — a sequence of statements — that is common to various makefiles we use. Then, whenever we need this particular sequence of statements, we tell NMAKE to include the file that contains them.

Let's look now at the `ifdef` directive. Remember that this directive asks NMAKE whether a particular macro has been defined. For our immediate interest, the directive

```
!ifdef DEBUG
```

asks NMAKE if a macro named `DEBUG` has been defined.

We can define the macro `DEBUG` in the makefile:

```
DEBUG  =  YES
```

(see Section 3.1.1, page 22). Or we can define the macro on the command line:

```
nmake  DEBUG=YES
```

(see Section 4.1, page 47).

If `DEBUG` is defined, NMAKE executes the statements between the `ifdef` and the `endif` directives. In our case, NMAKE would change `CFLAGS` to be defined as:

```
CFLAGS  =  -c  -W2  -Zi  -Od
```

It is important to notice that `CFLAGS` is left-justified on the line; that is, the C of `CFLAGS` appears below the `!`. We must begin `CFLAGS` in the first column of the line because it is a macro name, not a command.

Remember that only commands are indented on the line (with one or more spaces or tabs).

If DEBUG has not been defined, then NMAKE does not execute the statements between the **ifdef** and the **endif** directives; CFLAGS remains as originally defined.

Let's consider using the DEBUG macro in a different way. With the **if** and the **endif** directives, we can explicitly test whether DEBUG has been defined to be YES (or any other value we want to test for):

```
!if "$(DEBUG)" == "YES"

        ⋮

!endif
```

We can use an **else** directive following the **if** directive:

```
!if "$(DEBUG)" == "YES"

        ⋮

!else

        ⋮

!endif
```

This variation means that when DEBUG is defined to be YES, NMAKE executes the statements between the **if** and the **else** directives. When DEBUG is defined to be some value other than YES (or is not defined at all), NMAKE executes the statements between the **else** and the **endif** directives.

Let's add our debug flags to CFLAGS in the first case; let's keep CFLAGS simple in the second case:

```
!if "$(DEBUG)" == "YES"
CFLAGS =  -c  -W2  -Zi  -Od
!else
CFLAGS =  -c  -W2
!endif
```

Notice that in these examples of the **if** directive we use **$( )** around DEBUG and we use double quotation marks on both sides of the expression. (Contrast this notation with the earlier example of the **ifdef** directive where we used neither. We will return to this distinction in a minute.)

We must use **$( )** around DEBUG because we want the **if** directive to evaluate the *value* of DEBUG. Without **$( )**, **if** would compare the literal string "DEBUG" with the string "YES". The test, of course, fails — and is not what we intended in any event.

We must use the quotation marks because we have asked NMAKE to evaluate a comparison, and the values to be compared must be of the same type. In our case, the value we want to test, YES, is a string; this means that the other value, **$(DEBUG)**, must also be a string. We tell **if** to evaluate the comparison of two strings by surrounding each value with string delimiters (i.e., quotation marks). Without the quotation marks, **if** would expect to compare two integers.

Now let's consider the syntax of the **ifdef** directive. Recall that we used neither **$( )** nor quotation marks around DEBUG. This is because **ifdef** determines only whether the macro name has been defined; it does not check for the value of the macro nor does it require the macro name to be a particular type.

We can write more than one statement following an **if** or an **else** directive. For example, we may need to change the DOS environment variable INCLUDE to add a directory to the list of directories that the C preprocessor searches.

In our case, we want to add the \DEBUG directory to the INCLUDE environment variable when the macro DEBUG is assigned the value YES. Here are the lines we need in our makefile:

```
!if "$(DEBUG)" == "YES"
CFLAGS = -c -W2 -Zi -Od
!       if [set INCLUDE=%INCLUDE%;\DEBUG]
!       endif
!else
CFLAGS = -c -W2
!endif
```

Recall from Chapter 4 that we use the DOS **set** command to change the value of an environment variable. For NMAKE to perform this operation, the command must be within an **if** directive, where it always evaluates as nonzero. The brackets around the command are required, and the information within them

```
set INCLUDE=%INCLUDE%;\DEBUG
```

is passed directly to `command.com`.

We conclude this **if** directive right away with an **endif** because we do not have any other statements to execute after the **set** command.

From this brief discussion of preprocessing directives, we've gained some insight into their usefulness in makefiles. Different circumstances will suggest other uses. For more information about this versatile feature, refer to the online help that Microsoft provides with NMAKE.

5.4 Special Cases

We know from earlier chapters that when we construct and modify makefiles, we may need more than one line to specify a list of dependencies or a command with its various parameters. NMAKE accepts a backslash (\) before the end of a line as a signal that the current line has not ended. This means that the next line is the continuation of the line that ends with \.

This convention is helpful with long lines. This convention can also present a problem. For example, what will NMAKE do if it sees these lines in a makefile:

```
cd  \
copy  autoexec.bat  autoexec.old
```

The first command tells NMAKE to change to the root directory (in DOS, \ is the root directory for a device). Notice that this command ends with \, which is the last item on the line. Because \ means the root directory in DOS and NMAKE uses \ as a line continuation indicator, we have a problem. Specifically, NMAKE understands the command to be

```
cd  copy  autoexec.bat  autoexec.old
```

which is hardly what we had in mind!

Fortunately, we have a way to tell NMAKE when a \ is not meant to be a continuation indicator. We place a caret (^) in front of the backslash

```
cd  ^\
copy  autoexec.bat  autoexec.old
```

and NMAKE sees two command lines, as we intended.

The ^ turns off the special meaning — continuation indicator — for the backslash. This function of ^ extends to other characters in NMAKE. For example, the newline character signals the end of a line. If we want to use the newline as part of a string, we can turn off the meaning of newline by using a caret:

```
STRING=All^
is well.
```

We've defined the macro STRING to have two physical lines. Because ^ precedes the newline, STRING contains a newline after 'All'. When we display the contents of STRING, we'll see 'All' on one line followed by 'is well.' on the next line. If we do not use the ^ in front of the newline, NMAKE will understand the value of STRING to be 'All'. However, it will not recognize 'is well.' as anything meaningful and consequently will display an error message.

Alternatively, we can insert a newline in a string by specifying the newline character as \n. So the two physical lines we defined for STRING above become one line in the macro definition:

```
STRING=All\nis well.
```

In this case, of course, we do not need to use the ^ to turn off any special meanings. When we display the contents of STRING using this definition, we see two lines as we did before.

5.5   Creating Dependencies Dynamically

In Chapter 2 we mentioned the need for performing dependency checking. We are ready now to explore that concept further.

We well know by now that an important use of NMAKE is to maintain program modules within a development project. We also recall (from Chapter 2) that a source file may include other files.

We sometimes call these other files *header files* because they contain information that typically appears at the beginning, or head, of a program file. We also refer to these files as *include files*, for the obvious reason. In C language programs, the include (or header) files usually are recognizable by the .h extension to the file name; in assembler, the .inc extension is used. An include file may contain #define statements (C language) or equate statements (assembly language) that convey information to the file in which it is included.

Depending on the project, it may be more the rule than the exception that program modules use include files. To illustrate how this affects dependencies in a makefile, let's look again at the makefile we used in Chapter 3:

```
TARGET =  prog.exe
CFLAGS =  -W2  -O
OBJS   =  prog1.obj  prog2.obj

$(TARGET):  $(OBJS)
        $(CC)  -o  $@  $(OBJS)

prog1.obj:  prog1.c

prog2.obj:  prog2.c
```

(The lines with prog1.c and prog2.c ordinarily would not appear in the makefile because of .SUFFIXES: and the predefined inference rules, but we are showing them in this case for the purpose of illustrating the need for dependency checking.)

Based on this makefile, the only dependency for prog1.obj is prog1.c. But suppose that prog1.c uses the include file prog1.h. The relevant line in the makefile

```
prog1.obj:  prog1.c
```

gives no indication that prog1.h has anything to do with this dependency.

Now let's say that we have changed prog1.h — but not prog1.c — since the last time our makefile produced the .obj file for prog1.c. Because prog1.c includes prog1.h, we want NMAKE to recompile prog1.c when either it or prog1.h is modified. But NMAKE does not know this. In this situation, NMAKE does not know to check the date and time of prog1.h. It checks only the date and time of prog1.obj and of prog1.c and does not recompile prog1.c until prog1.c is modified.

An obvious solution to the apparent dilemma presents itself. We need simply to change our makefile to show that prog1.obj depends on both files:

```
prog1.obj:  prog1.c  prog1.h
```

It is clear now that `prog1.h` is a direct dependency for `prog1.obj`.

It is vital, as this example shows, that we state all the dependencies for every file we need to work with in the makefile.

The importance of this requirement cannot be overstated; however, it is not always easy to remember every include file in every program module. But consider this: what if we devise some way to have NMAKE help us to satisfy the requirement?

The tool we have in mind is a program that creates a correct — and complete — list of dependencies for the makefile. Still working with the example from Chapter 3, our program will have to read the two identified indirect dependencies, `prog1.c` and `prog2.c`, and look for include files within them. The output of the program will be the original makefile plus a dependency list for each `.obj` file. Then any time we modify either of the `.c` files, we will rerun the program to create an updated dependency list.

We have, in fact, developed such a tool: the program **depends** in Appendix E builds a dependency list from the dependencies stated in the makefile. The program reads the current makefile to collect the object file names (i.e., `prog1.obj` and `prog2.obj`). **depends** then reads each source program (it looks for `.c` and `.asm` files for a given `.obj` target), looking for **include** statements, and updates the makefile to reflect the current dependency list.

We must make some changes to our makefile if we want to use **depends** to accomplish automatic dependency checking. Here is the modified makefile:

```
CFLAGS  =  -c  -W2  -O

prog.exe:  prog1.obj  prog2.obj
        $(CC)  -o  $@  prog1.obj  prog2.obj

dependen:
        copy  makefile  makefile.old
        depends  -I.  -I%%INCLUDE%%  >makefile
        $(MAKE)
```

Let's investigate the changes we made. First, we removed the dependency lines

```
prog1.obj:   prog1.c
prog2.obj:   prog2.c
```

because **depends** will generate them. We also created a pseudotarget, **dependen**, with three command lines:

```
copy  makefile  makefile.old
depends  -I.  -I%%INCLUDE%%  >makefile
$(MAKE)
```

The **copy** command makes a backup copy of **makefile**. We save a copy of the makefile in **makefile.old** just in case something does not work the way we expect it to work. (Another reason is that **depends** reads the input from a default file named **makefile.old**. See Appendix E for information about naming the input file.)

The **depends** command executes the **depends** program using a few options. (The options are explained in Appendix E.) We redirect the output from **depends** (the original makefile and the dependency list) to the current makefile; that is, we overwrite the existing makefile. Finally, because the predefined macro **MAKE** expands to the **nmake** command, NMAKE is invoked recursively. One note about the options for **depends**: we use %% around the environment variable INCLUDE because **depends** expects to find an environment variable surrounded by %s, as in %INCLUDE%. To NMAKE, % is a special character so we must use two %s to mean one %. Using -I%%INCLUDE%% allows us to pass -I%INCLUDE% to **depends**.

Now, to build the dependency list, we invoke **nmake** on the command line and specify the target:

```
nmake  dependen
```

Here is the makefile after **depends** modifies it:

```
CFLAGS  =  -c  -W2  -O

prog.exe:  prog1.obj  prog2.obj
           $(CC)  -o  $@  prog1.obj  prog2.obj

dependen:
           copy  makefile  makefile.old
           depends  -I.  -I%%INCLUDE%%  >makefile
           $(MAKE)

prog1.obj:  prog1.c        \
            f:\c600\include\stdio.h             \
            .\prog1.h
prog2.obj:  prog2.c        \
            f:\c600\include\stdio.h
```

depends determined that **prog1.c** includes two files, **stdio.h** and **prog1.h**, and that **prog2.c** includes only one, **stdio.h**.

We can see that the job of building the dependency list for a makefile is much easier when we use a program like **depends**.

Let's review how this works. From the command line we execute

nmake dependen

which causes NMAKE to begin executing the makefile at the pseudotarget **dependen**. NMAKE then makes a backup copy of the makefile, creates the dependency list, and writes it to **makefile**. When NMAKE reaches the third command line for the pseudotarget, it reinvokes itself and begins executing the same makefile from the top. This second instance of NMAKE finds **prog.exe** to be the first target in the makefile, so it begins to do all the things necessary to build **prog.exe**. Note that in this instance NMAKE does not execute the commands associated with the pseudotarget because **dependen** is not required for **prog.exe**. NMAKE does, however, find the dependency lines for **prog1.obj** and **prog2.obj** because **depends** inserted them on the first instance of NMAKE.

NMAKE does not find **dependen** the second time because that target is not part of **prog.exe** and we are not explicitly referring to that pseudotarget. The only way we reach **dependen:** is by using the target name on the command line.

5.6   NMAKE and the tools.ini File

The latest version of the Microsoft C compiler provides for a special file, called `tools.ini`, which NMAKE can use. When we invoke NMAKE, before it begins to execute the makefile it first reads `tools.ini` (when the file is present) and uses the macros and inference rules it finds there. There is an exception to this general rule: if a makefile and `tools.ini` both contain a definition for a macro with the same name or an inference rule with the same extensions, the definition in the makefile overrides the definition in `tools.ini`.

NMAKE looks for `tools.ini` in the current directory. If `tools.ini` is not in the current directory, we can use the `set` command to create an environment variable called INIT. (We learned about environment variables and the `set` command in Chapter 4.) We can define INIT to specify the path to the directory that contains initialization files, including `tools.ini`. Now NMAKE can find `tools.ini` by searching the directory that INIT specifies.

We can use `tools.ini` to customize default options for NMAKE. Suppose, for example, that we want to use a file with the extension `.inc` to create another file with the extension `.tex`. We can create an inference rule so NMAKE knows how to perform this task for us:

```
.inc.tex:
        include  <$*.inc >$*.tex
```

If we need this rule in several different makefiles, we can omit the rule from the individual makefiles and add it to `tools.ini`:

```
[NMAKE]
.inc.tex:
        include  <$*.inc >$*.tex
```

Thus, we can use `tools.ini` the same way we use the `include` directive, which we learned about earlier. Is one technique preferred over the other? In terms of results, no; they are the same. However, consider this: If we use the preprocessor directive, we must not only create another file, we must also remember to put the `include` statement in the makefile. NMAKE, on the other hand, looks for and reads `tools.ini` automatically, requiring no extra effort on our part.

The online help information from Microsoft provides more specific details about the `tools.ini` file and how to use it.

5.7 Macro Precedence

A macro defined on the command line has the highest precedence in NMAKE. At the next level of precedence are macros defined in the makefile. A macro defined in the makefile has precedence over inherited macros. (Inherited macros are macros that are equivalent to every environment variable. NMAKE makes a copy of environment variables and gives them uppercase names.) At the next level below inherited macros are macros defined in the `tools.ini` file, followed by predefined macros.

For example, if a macro name appears in `tools.ini`, then NMAKE will use the value for that macro from `tools.ini` as long as a macro with the same name does not appear either on the command line or in the makefile and is not an inherited macro.

Let's consider a specific case. `CFLAGS` is a predefined macro that we discussed in Chapter 3. NMAKE will use its predefined value only if `CFLAGS` does not appear on the command line, is not defined in the makefile, is not an inherited macro, and does not appear in `tools.ini`. This is because predefined macros have the lowest precedence in NMAKE.

5.8 Summary

NMAKE supports an extensive list of command line options. A number of these options are unique to NMAKE. Refer to page 66 for a list of options.

NMAKE also supports preprocessing directives. These directives allow us to control the operation of NMAKE with conditional and other special-purpose statements. A preprocessing directive begins with ! in the first column of the line on which it appears. NMAKE processes any directives it finds in the makefile before executing the commands associated with targets.

Two frequently used directives are `ifdef` and `if`. Both `ifdef` and `if` must be followed by an `endif` directive; and both directives can use the `else` directive to establish alternative action for NMAKE to take.

The `ifdef` directive determines whether the name that follows it has been defined for the current makefile. The `if` directive evaluates the expression that follows it (`if` *expr*) and executes the statements until the `endif` or `else` when *expr* is nonzero. A special use of the `if` directive is to pass a command directly to `command.com`. In this case, the command to be passed must be enclosed in [ ].

The caret (^) is a special control character that turns off the special meaning of other characters. When used before a backslash (^\), it tells NMAKE that the backslash is a literal character and not a line continuation indicator. Similarly, when used in a macro definition before a newline character, the ^ tells NMAKE that the newline is part of the definition, not an end-of-line marker for NMAKE. Another way to represent the newline character without having to use ^ is to use \n where the newline should occur.

A complete and correct list of dependencies is critical to the successful operation of NMAKE. Source files that NMAKE uses to build a target often contain header files (.h) or include files (.inc), which can easily be omitted from a makefile, usually with unwanted (if not disastrous) results. Dependency checking can be performed dynamically as NMAKE executes to ensure that all dependencies are known to NMAKE. Refer to Appendix E for an example of a program that produces an accurate, up-to-date list of dependencies for a makefile.

The latest version of the Microsoft C compiler provides for a special file, called `tools.ini`. We can add macro definitions and inference rules to this file for NMAKE to use. However, if a makefile and the `tools.ini` file contain conflicting definitions or rules, NMAKE uses the makefile in preference to `tools.ini`. Because NMAKE reads `tools.ini` automatically, it provides a convenient device for customizing default options for NMAKE.

The precedence of macros, from highest (1) to lowest (5) is:

1. macros on the command line

2. macros in the makefile

3. inherited macros

4. macros in the `tools.ini` file

5. predefined macros

Chapter 6

Borland's MAKE

In previous chapters we looked at concepts and strategies that, for the most part, apply universally to all versions of *make*. Here we focus our attention on the *make* utility MAKE from Borland.

We begin this chapter by showing how to invoke MAKE. Then we explore topics that apply specifically to Borland's MAKE. Some of these topics — options, dependencies, and continuation lines — we met earlier. New topics introduced in this chapter are preprocessor directives and the `builtins.mak` file, the second of which is unique to MAKE.

6.1 Invoking MAKE

Here is the format for invoking MAKE on the command line:

```
make [options] [targets]
```

The brackets ([ ]) around a field name indicate that the field is optional. Thus, the two fields are optional for MAKE.

6.2 Command Line Options

MAKE supports an extensive list of command line options. If you are familiar with other versions of *make*, some of these options may look familiar. However, a number of MAKE options differ from those supported in other versions of *make*.

MAKE is case sensitive with respect to options; that is, MAKE treats s and S as two different options. Remember that when we specify an

81

option on the command line, we must precede the option letter with a dash (-) or a forward slash (/). Notice that when an option takes an argument, we do not put any space between the option and the argument.

Here are the options that MAKE supports:

a	Perform automatic dependency check on all `.obj` files
B	Build all targets regardless of time stamp (file dates)
D*identifier*	Define the value of *identifier* to be 1
D*identifier=string*	Define the value of *identifier* to be *string*
f*filename*	Specify the makefile to be *filename*
h	Display help information
i	Ignore exit/error codes
I*directory*	Search for include files in *directory*
K	Retain any temporary file(s) created by MAKE
n	Display commands but do not execute them
s	Suppress command display while executing
S	Swap MAKE out of memory while executing commands
U*identifier*	Undefine *identifier* if previously defined
W	Write the current specified non-string options to `make.exe`
?	Display help information

6.3 Preprocessing Directives

A preprocessing directive is a command or an instruction that allows us to conditionally execute other commands or to conditionally select parts of a makefile. When *make* reads a makefile, it processes any preprocessing directives it finds before it executes commands associated with targets.

A preprocessing directive begins with an exclamation mark (!) and must appear at the beginning of the line. That is, we must place the ! in the first column on the line. However, after the ! we can use blank spaces and/or tabs, if we wish, to enhance readability of the file.

Here are the preprocessing directives that MAKE supports:

error *message*	Display error message
include "*filename*"	Insert another file as part of this makefile
if *expr*	Execute statements following **if** when *expr* evaluates to nonzero
elif *expr*	Execute statements following **elif** when the preceding **if** evaluates to zero and this *expr* evaluates to nonzero
else	Execute statements following **else** when *expr* in the preceding **if** (and in the preceding **elif**, when present) evaluates to zero
endif	Mark the end of an **if** directive
undef *name*	Undefine *name* (same as the U*identifier* option on the command line)

To see how we can apply preprocessing directives, let's start with a variation of a makefile from Chapter 3. We've adapted the makefile to work with Borland's MAKE. Here is the modified makefile:

```
# Define Macros

EXEC_NAME       =  prog
CC              =  tcc
CFLAGS          =  -c -ms
OBJS            =  prog1.obj  prog2.obj

# Define Inference Rules

.c.obj:
        $(CC)  $(CFLAGS)  $*.c

# Target and Dependencies

$(EXEC_NAME).exe:  $(OBJS)
        $(CC)  -e$<  $(OBJS)
```

Now let's modify the makefile to use directives. Here is what we want to achieve:

- Include another makefile (called `sample.mak`) as part of our makefile. The macros we want to use will be defined in this file.

- Use the `$d` predefined macro (which tests for a defined macro) to determine if some action should be performed (see next item).

- If the `DEBUG` macro has been defined, add the `-O-` and `-r-` compiler options to CFLAGS (`-O-` indicates that we want to disable optimization; `-r-` tells `tcc` to suppress the use of register variables).

Here is the makefile in its new form:

```
# Include the file sample.mak

!include  "sample.mak"

# Define Inference Rules

.c.obj:
        $(CC)  $(CFLAGS)  $*.c

# Test for defined macro

!if $d(DEBUG)
CFLAGS          = $(CFLAGS)  -O-  -r-
!endif

# Target and Dependencies

$(EXEC_NAME).exe:  $(OBJS)
        $(CC)  -e$<  $(OBJS)
```

Let's look more closely at the new features of this makefile, beginning with the **include** directive. We have used the **include** directive

```
    !include  "sample.mak"
```

to tell *make* to read the file **sample.mak** into the current makefile. When *make* begins to process the makefile, it appears as if the contents of **sample.mak** were always present. Effectively, they are: the directive brings them in. Here are the contents of **sample.mak**:

```
# Define Macros

EXEC_NAME       = prog
CC              = tcc
CFLAGS          = -c -ms
OBJS            = prog1.obj  prog2.obj
```

By using the **include** directive, we can easily create part of a makefile — a sequence of statements — that is common to various makefiles we use. Then, whenever we need this particular sequence of statements, we tell *make* to include the file that contains them.

Let's look now at how we've used the **if** directive. Remember that this directive asks *make* to evaluate an expression; that is, to determine whether the expression is true (the return value is nonzero) or false (the return value is zero). For our immediate interest, the directive statement

```
!if $d(DEBUG)
```

asks *make* whether a macro named DEBUG has been defined (Notice that the predefined macro $d uses a d — not a D — and should not be confused with the D*identifier* option from the command line. Remember that MAKE is case sensitive.)

We can define the macro DEBUG in the makefile:

```
DEBUG  =  3
```

(see Section 3.1.1, page 22). Or we can define the macro on the command line using the D*identifier* option:

```
make   -DDEBUG=3
```

(see Section 4.1, page 47).

If DEBUG is defined, *make* executes the statements between the **if** and the **endif** directives. In our case, *make* would change CFLAGS to be defined as:

```
CFLAGS  =  -c -ms -0- -r-
```

It is important to notice that CFLAGS is left-justified on the line; that is, the C of CFLAGS appears below the **!**. We must begin CFLAGS in the first column of the line because it is a macro name, not a command. Remember that only commands are indented on the line (with one or more spaces or tabs).

If DEBUG is not defined, then *make* does not execute the statements between the **if** and the **endif** directives; CFLAGS remains as originally defined.

Let's consider using the DEBUG macro in a different way. With the **if** and the **endif** directives, we can explicitly test whether DEBUG has been defined to be 3 (or any other value we want to test for):

```
!if $(DEBUG) == 3

        :

!endif
```

We can use an **else** directive following the **if** directive:

```
!if $(DEBUG) == 3

    ⋮

!else

    ⋮

!endif
```

This variation means that when DEBUG is defined to be 3, *make* executes the statements between the if and the else directives. When DEBUG is defined to be some value other than 3 (or has not been defined at all), *make* executes the statements between the else and the endif directives.

Let's add our debug flags to CFLAGS in the first case; let's keep CFLAGS simple in the second case:

```
!if $(DEBUG) == 3
CFLAGS  =  -c  -ms  -O-  -r-
!else
CFLAGS  =  -c  -ms
!endif
```

Notice that in these examples of the if directive we use $( ) around DEBUG. This is because we are interested in the value of the macro DEBUG, and the notation that tells *make* to use the value of a macro is $( ).

Now let's consider a variation on our earlier directive statement:

```
!if !$d(DEBUG)
```

With this if directive using the $d predefined macro, we are asking *make* to evaluate whether the DEBUG macro is defined. More specifically, by using the syntax shown above, we are checking for the non-existence of the macro (the second ! in the statement is a NOT operator). In other words, if DEBUG is not defined, *make* will return a true (i.e., nonzero) value to the preprocessing directive.

As with any if statement, we can use the results of this evaluation to conditionally perform some specific task. In the following example, the action *make* takes is based on whether the macro DEBUG has or has not been defined:

```
!if !$d(DEBUG)
DEBUG  =  3
!endif
```

If the macro already is defined, the expression evaluates to false, and *make* ignores the new definition given between the **if** and **endif** directives. However, if the macro is not defined, the condition given to the **if** directive evaluates to true, and *make* defines the macro with the value 3.

We can write more than one statement following an **if** or an **else** directive. For example,

```
!if $d(DEBUG)
CFLAGS  =  -c  -ms  -O-  -r-
MESSAGE = "DEBUG has been defined"
!else
CFLAGS  =  -c
MESSAGE = "DEBUG has NOT been defined"
!       if !$d(MODEL)
CFLAGS  =  -ms  $(CFLAGS)
!       else
CFLAGS  =  -m$(MODEL)  $(CFLAGS)
!       endif
!endif
```

In this example we are testing first whether the DEBUG macro has been defined. If DEBUG has been defined, we assign one set of compiler options to CFLAGS and we assign a string to MESSAGE; otherwise, we define CFLAGS for a different set of options, we assign a different string to MESSAGE, and we test whether the MODEL macro has been defined.

Notice we have an **if** within an **if** (nested **if** statements) when we test whether the MODEL macro has been defined. In this case, if MODEL has not been defined, we add the ms compiler option to the value previously assigned to the CFLAGS macro; otherwise, the compiler option we add reflects the value already assigned to MODEL.

This example highlights two additional points of interest. First, each **if** directive must conclude with its own corresponding **endif** directive. Second, as long as we place the ! in the first column of the line, we can use spaces or tabs to enhance readability.

Now let's make some more changes to the makefile to further illustrate the use of directives. This time our criteria are:

- Look in the current directory for the source files.

- Put the object files in a subdirectory called sample2 (we will use the o compiler option to accomplish this).

- If the DEBUG macro is defined, change the compiler options to include debug information. Otherwise, use the value of CFLAGS as defined in the include file sample.mak.

To meet these criteria, we change our makefile so it looks like this:

```
.PATH.c    =   .
.PATH.obj =   .\sample2

OBJS = $(.PATH.obj)\prog1.obj $(.PATH.obj)\prog2.obj

!include    "sample.mak"

!if $d(DEBUG)
CFLAGS     =  $(CFLAGS)  -O-  -r-
!endif

# Define Inference Rules

.c.obj:
      $(CC) $(CFLAGS) -o$(.PATH.obj)\$*.obj $*.c

# Target and Dependencies

$(EXEC_NAME).exe:  $(OBJS)
      $(CC)  -e$<  $(OBJS)
```

Now let's look at the changes we've made. First, we added two .PATH statements. These statements tell *make* the paths to use when searching for files with the .c extension and the .obj extension; specifically, the .c files for this makefile are in the current directory, and the .obj files are in a subdirectory called sample2.

Next, we changed the OBJS macro. We redefined OBJS to tell *make* that the path for the object files is not the current directory, but is the directory defined for .PATH.obj.

Finally, we changed the compiler command line associated with the inference rule for building .obj files from .c files. Now when *make* compiles a .c file, it places the output (that is, the .obj file) in the directory defined for .PATH.obj.

From this discussion of preprocessing directives, we've gained some insight into their usefulness in makefiles. Different circumstances will suggest other uses. For more information about this versatile feature, refer to the documentation that Borland provides for MAKE.

6.4   Continuation Lines

Unlike other versions of the *make* utility, Borland's MAKE does not support escape sequences. This fact sets up an interesting situation.

We already know that a backslash (\) at the end of a line tells *make* that the next line in the makefile is a continuation of the line on which the \ occurs. Suppose, however, that we want to copy a file created in our makefile to the root directory of the system (which also is represented by \).

How does *make* know the difference between the case where \ indicates a continuation line

```
prog1.obj: prog1.c     \
        prog1.h
```

and the case where it does not:

```
copy $< \
```

The answer, fortunately, is simple: we can use a double backslash (\\) to tell *make* that it should see a literal \ and not a line continuation indicator. Thus, when *make* sees

```
copy $< \\
```

it knows to copy the file represented by $< to the root directory.

6.5 Creating Dependencies Dynamically

In Chapter 2 we mentioned the need for performing dependency checking. We are ready now to explore that concept further.

We well know by now that an important use of *make* is to maintain program modules within a development project. We also recall (from Chapter 2) that a source file may include other files.

We sometimes call these other files *header files* because they contain information that typically appears at the beginning, or head, of a program file. We also refer to these files as *include files*, for the obvious reason. In C language programs, the header (or include) files usually are recognizable by the .h extension to the file name; in assembler, the .inc extension is used. An include file may contain #define statements (C language) or equate statements (assembly language) that convey information to the file in which it is included.

Depending on the project, it may be more the rule than the exception that program modules use include files. To illustrate how this affects dependencies in a makefile, let's look again at the Borland version of the makefile we used at the beginning of this chapter:

```
# Define Macros

EXEC_NAME        =  prog
CC               =  tcc
CFLAGS           =  -c -ms
OBJS             =  prog1.obj  prog2.obj

# Define Inference Rules

.c.obj:
        $(CC)  $(CFLAGS) $*.c

# Target and Dependencies

$(EXEC_NAME).exe:  $(OBJS)
        $(CC)  -e$<  $(OBJS)
```

(The lines with `prog1.c` and `prog2.c` ordinarily would not appear in the makefile because of the inference rule, but we are showing them in this case for the purpose of illustrating the need for dependency checking.)

Based on this makefile, the only dependency for `prog1.obj` is `prog1.c`. But suppose that `prog1.c` uses the include file `prog1.h`. The relevant line in the makefile

```
    prog1.obj:  prog1.c
```

gives no indication that `prog1.h` has anything to do with this dependency.

Now let's say that we have changed `prog1.h` — but not `prog1.c` — since the last time our makefile produced the `.obj` file for `prog1.c`. Because `prog1.c` includes `prog1.h`, we want *make* to recompile `prog1.c` when either it or `prog1.h` is modified. But *make* does not know this. In this situation, *make* does not know to check the date and time of `prog1.h`. It checks only the date and time of `prog1.obj` and of `prog1.c` and does not recompile `prog1.c` until `prog1.c` is modified.

An obvious solution to the apparent dilemma presents itself. We need simply to change our makefile to show that `prog1.obj` depends on both files:

```
    prog1.obj:  prog1.c  prog1.h
```

It is clear now that `prog1.h` is a direct dependency for `prog1.obj`.

It is vital, as this example shows, that we state all the dependencies for every file we need to work with in the makefile.

The importance of this requirement cannot be overstated; however, it is not always easy to remember every include file in every program module. But because we are using the Borland version of the *make* utility, we are in luck!

One of the features Borland provides is the availability of built-in dependency checking for all source files. Recall from page 82 that the **a** option instructs *make* to perform dependency checking for us. When we use this option, the source programs are checked for include files and an internal dependency list is created for *make* to use. The makefile itself does not change, unless we use the K option along with the a option. (Remember that the K option tells *make* to keep the temporary files it creates; otherwise, they are automatically removed.)

Thus, to build a complete and accurate dependency list for our makefile, we specify the **a** option when we invoke *make*:

```
make  -a
```

Because we issued the `make` command with this option, *make* determines whether any source files contain include files (and, if so, searches the current directory and the directories listed in the `INCLUDE` environment variable), then builds the `.obj` targets accordingly.

We can see, then, that the job of building the dependency list for any makefile is much easier to accomplish when we use the **a** option. This option is so helpful, in fact, that we are well-advised to use it liberally.

6.6 MAKE and the builtins.mak File

make supports the use of a general file called `builtins.mak`. When we issue the `make` command, it automatically searches for this special file and, if it is present, includes the file as part of the makefile currently being executed. However, *make* does not require `builtins.mak` to exist.

The `builtins.mak` feature provides a tool we can use to supplement the limited set of predefined macros that MAKE supports. We can also use this file to develop and maintain a set of inference rules (remember that *make* does not have any predefined inference rules).

To make use of this feature, we create the file `builtins.mak`, which should reside in the same directory as `make.exe`, and include in it the

macros and rules we want to use over and over again. We can illustrate
this idea by making a few changes to our previous makefile. We will
remove the **include** directive and the inference rule and put them into
builtins.mak. (Remember that once we remove the **include** directive,
make does not know about the **sample.mak** file or its contents.)

Here is our new makefile:

```
.PATH.c   =   .
.PATH.obj =   .\sample2

OBJS = $(.PATH.obj)\prog1.obj $(.PATH.obj)\prog2.obj

!if $d(DEBUG)
CFLAGS  =  $(CFLAGS)  -O-  -r-
!endif

# Target and Dependencies

$(EXEC_NAME).exe:  $(OBJS)
     $(CC)  -e$<  $(OBJS)
```

We see that this makefile still relies on the macros **EXEC_NAME**, **CC**, and
CFLAGS; however, they are not defined in the makefile (we are assuming
that the **DEBUG** macro was defined on the command line). Furthermore,
we want *make* to build .obj files from .c files, but we have not provided
any rules for doing so. Nor have we told *make* to include the contents of
any other file that might contain this information.

How, then, does *make* know what to do? Simply by reading the
builtins.mak file, which we wrote to include the following lines:

```
EXEC_NAME    =  prog
CC           =  tcc
CFLAGS       =  -c  -ms

.c.obj:
          $(CC) $(CFLAGS) -o$(.PATH.obj)\$* $*.c
```

The technique of using **builtins.mak** works exactly like the **include**
directive with one significant difference: the lines in **builtins.mak** will
be used in every makefile executed by *make* on our system, instead of only
in those makefiles in which we remember to use the **include** directive.

6.7 Macro Precedence

If a macro has been defined in `builtins.mak`, then *make* uses that definition. If the same macro is redefined in the makefile, the latest definition takes effect.

A macro can be defined on the command line using the D*identifier* option. If we redefine the same macro in the makefile, that is considered its latest definition; again, the latest definition takes effect.

If a macro is defined on the command line and is redefined in `builtins.mak`, the redefinition from `builtins.mak` takes effect.

The order of precedence for macros in Borland's MAKE is simple: the last definition of the macro that MAKE sees is the definition that takes effect.

6.8 Summary

The *make* utility from Borland supports an extensive list of command line options. A number of these options are unique to MAKE. Refer to page 82 for a list of options.

make also supports preprocessing directives. These directives allow us to control the operation of *make* with conditional and other special-purpose statements. A preprocessing directive begins with ! in the first column of the line on which it appears. *make* processes any directives it finds in the makefile before executing the commands associated with targets.

One frequently used directive is the `if` directive. The statement(s) associated with this directive must be followed by an `endif` directive. The `if` directive can also use both the `elif` and the `else` directives to establish alternative action for *make* to take.

When followed by the name of a macro, the `if` directive determines whether that macro has been defined for the current makefile. The predefined macro `$d` can be used in conjunction with the `if` directive to test a macro; its use can be extended with the NOT operator (!) to test that a macro has not been defined.

make recognizes \ as a line continuation indicator. The root directory on DOS is represented by \. To avoid confusion as to whether \ indicates the continuation of a line or represents the root directory, we use \\ for the latter.

A complete and correct list of dependencies is critical to the successful operation of *make*. Source files that *make* uses to build a target often contain header files (`.h`) or include files (`.inc`), which can easily be omitted from a makefile, usually with unwanted (if not disastrous) results. The **a** option makes it possible for dependency checking to be performed dynamically as *make* executes to ensure that all dependencies are known to *make*.

make supports a special file called `builtins.mak`. We can use this file to hold macros and inference rules that we define and want to use frequently. Because *make* reads `builtins.mak` automatically, it provides a convenient device for customizing default options for *make*.

The precedence of macros, from highest (1) to lowest (3) is:

1. macros in the makefile

2. macros in the `builtins.mak` file

3. macros on the command line

Chapter 7

UNIX System's MAKE

In previous chapters we looked at concepts and strategies that, for the most part, apply universally to all versions of *make*. Here we focus our attention on the MAKE utility on UNIX systems.

We begin this chapter by showing how to invoke MAKE. Then we explore several topics that were introduced earlier as they apply specifically to MAKE on UNIX systems. For example, we will revisit options, environment variables, predefined macros, and inference rules in the UNIX environment.

7.1 Invoking MAKE

Here is the format for invoking MAKE on the command line:

```
make  [options]  [macro_definitions]  [targets]
```

The brackets ([ ]) around a field name indicate that the field is optional. Thus, all three fields are optional for MAKE.

7.2 Command Line Options

MAKE supports an extensive list of command line options. If you are familiar with other versions of *make*, some of these options may look familiar. However, a number of MAKE options differ from those supported in other versions of *make*.

MAKE is case sensitive with respect to options; that is, MAKE treats **s** and **S** as two different options. Remember that when we specify an

option on the command line, we must precede the option letter with a
dash (-).

Here are some of the options that MAKE supports:

d   Debug mode: print detailed information about the files
            being examined

e   Let environment variables override macro definitions

f *filename*   Specify makefile to be *filename*

i   Ignore exit/error codes

n   Display commands but do not execute them

p   Print values of defined macros and pseudotargets

q   Return exit code

r   Do not use built-in rules

s   Suppress command display while executing

t   Change target modification dates

7.3   Makefile Command Lines

A target can have any number of command lines. For MAKE on UNIX
systems, a command line in a makefile must begin with a tab character.
(In this respect, this version of *make* differs from the versions of *make*
that run on DOS systems, where command lines may begin with either a
tab or a space character.)

MAKE starts a separate process for each command line in the
makefile. Most of the time this characteristic does not affect the execution
of the commands. There is one case, however, that we need to be aware of.
Let's consider a makefile with some target that contains the two command
lines:

```
cd   somedir
ls
```

The first command tells MAKE to change to a new directory called `somedir`. However, MAKE runs a separate process to execute this command. The second command, `ls`, tells MAKE to list the files in the current directory. Because each command line runs as a separate process, the `cd` command does not affect subsequent lines. That is, in the UNIX system, MAKE issues `cd somedir` in a separate shell and waits for its completion. This separate shell does not affect the current shell where MAKE issues the `ls` command. Consequently, the `ls` command refers to the files in the current directory, *not* the files in `somedir`.

How can we get around this apparent limitation? If we replace the two command lines shown above with the single command line

```
cd  somedir;  ls
```

MAKE runs one process that consists of two commands: `cd  somedir`, and `ls`. Now the `ls` command refers to the files in `somedir`. After the process for this command line terminates, MAKE is back in the directory where it was before it executed the `cd somedir` command.

Another way to indicate that a command continues on the next line (and, therefore, is part of the same process) is to use the backslash character (\):

```
cd somedir; \
ls
```

Note that the UNIX system still requires the semicolon (;) between multiple commands to be executed in the same process, regardless whether the commands are on one physical line in the makefile or on several lines with \ line continuation indicators.

7.4 Environment Variables

MAKE reads the environment variables before it reads the file that contains the macros, targets, and commands (in UNIX systems, the default file MAKE uses is either `makefile` or `Makefile`). Therefore, we can override an environment variable by assigning a new value to the variable in the makefile.

MAKE uses the environment variable `MAKEFLAGS` to remember input options. `MAKEFLAGS` remembers input options through the lifetime of the current `make` command. This means that when we use MAKE recursively (as we discussed in Chapter 4), any option that we specified in the initial invocation of MAKE remains in effect via the `MAKEFLAGS` variable for all subsequent instances of MAKE.

For example, when we invoke MAKE with the n option, we tell MAKE to show the commands that would be executed, but without executing them. That is true, with one exception: when MAKE finds the `MAKE` macro, MAKE re-invokes itself, and continues to check and report the lines that should be executed for the second instance of MAKE. This behavior of n violates the general rule that MAKE does not *execute* the commands. The reason for this exception is that MAKE needs to follow a recursion or a hierarchy of makefiles to determine all the commands that will be executed when we invoke MAKE without the n option.

7.5   Macros and Macro Precedence

The MAKE utility in UNIX systems supports more predefined macros than the DOS versions of *make*. Remember the p option? When we invoke MAKE with this option

```
make  -p
```

MAKE displays all predefined macros, inference rules, and environment variables (even when we do not have a makefile present). Try it on your system.

Here is a subset of the predefined macros in our UNIX system:

```
ASFLAGS =
AS      = as
CFLAGS  = -O
CC      = cc
LDFLAGS =
LD      = ld
LFLAGS  =
LEX     = lex
YFLAGS  =
YACC    = yacc
MAKE    = make
```

We chose to show you these predefined macros because they are similar to those in Microsoft's *make* utility NMAKE. Four of these predefined

macros may be unfamiliar to you: LEX and YACC and the associated
flags macros are unique to the UNIX system's MAKE. These macros
are defined to invoke the lex and yacc tools that are available on UNIX
systems.

There are many more macros. Use the p option and consult your
UNIX system documentation to determine which ones are available on
your system.

On UNIX systems, a macro defined on the command line has
precedence over all other macros in MAKE. At the next level of precedence
are macros defined in the makefile. A macro defined in the makefile has
precedence over environment variables and predefined macros. Finally,
an environment variable has precedence over predefined macros.

For example, if a macro name appears in the environment, then the
UNIX system's MAKE uses the value of the environment variable as long
as a macro with the same name does not appear either on the command
line or in the makefile.

Let's consider a specific case. CFLAGS is a predefined macro that we
discussed in Chapter 3. If CFLAGS does not appear on the command line,
in the makefile, or in the environment, then MAKE uses its predefined
value. However, if we redefine the value of CFLAGS at any of these levels,
MAKE ignores the predefined value and uses the new definition. This is
because predefined macros have the lowest precedence in MAKE.

7.6 Suffixes and Inference Rules

In the UNIX systems we have used, the MAKE utility knows more
suffixes and has more built-in inference rules than Microsoft's NMAKE
or Borland's MAKE. When we run

```
make  -p
```

MAKE lists predefined macros, suffixes, and built-in inference rules.

The list of suffixes that MAKE knows is rather long. Here is the
predefined pseudotarget .SUFFIXES: as it is defined on one UNIX system:

```
.SUFFIXES: .o  .c  .c~  .y  .y~  .l  .l~  .s  .s~   \
       .sh  .sh~  .h  .h~  .out  .F  .f  .e  .r    \
       .yr  .ye  .cl  .p
```

The extensions followed by ˜ (for example, `.c˜`) refer to Source Code
Control System (SCCS) files. Consult your UNIX system documentation
for an explanation of any extensions that may be unfamiliar to you. (Note
that `.SUFFIXES:` does not contain continuation lines; we've added them
here to split a long line.)

Here are some of the built-in inference rules that MAKE knows:

```
.c.o:
        $(CC) $(CFLAGS) -c $<


.s.o:
        $(AS) $(ASFLAGS) -o $@ $<


.c:
        $(CC) $(CFLAGS) $(LDFLAGS) $< -o $@
```

Let's examine the inference rules a little more closely. Recall that
UNIX systems use `.o` for object files (in contrast to DOS, which uses the
`.obj` extension). The command line associated with the `.c.o:` inference
rule is:

```
$(CC) $(CFLAGS) -c $<
```

This command line indicates that MAKE will invoke the C compiler
with the value of `CFLAGS` and the `-c` compiler option to compile the current
target (represented by the predefined macro `$<`) to obtain an object file.
The `.s.o:` inference rule similarly applies to building object files from
assembly language files.

The last inference rule listed above

```
.c:
        $(CC) $(CFLAGS) $(LDFLAGS) $< -o $@
```

does not look like any of the inference rules we've seen so far. Most
noticeably it contains only one extension (`.c:`). This is called a *null suffix*
because MAKE assumes an empty (null) suffix between the `.c` extension
and the colon (`:`). This is the rule MAKE uses to build an executable
file from a `.c` file. (Remember that UNIX systems do not have a specific
extension for executable files, unlike DOS, which uses either the `.exe` or
the `.com` extension for executable files.)

The benefit we derive from the `.c:` inference rule is that we do not
have to create a makefile to compile a program that appears in one source

file. For example, if we have a file called `prog.c` that contains a program and its associated functions, we can issue the command

```
make   prog
```

even though we have not created a makefile with the `prog:` target. When MAKE executes this command, it applies the built-in `.c:` inference rule, compiles `prog.c`, and produces an executable file `prog`. (We are assuming, of course, that `prog.c` does not contain any syntax errors.) This is a quick and easy way to produce an executable file from a single source file.

When you use the p option with MAKE, you will see more inference rules. Try the p option on your system and consult your UNIX system documentation.

7.7 Summary

The MAKE utility on UNIX systems supports an extensive list of command line options. A number of these options are unique to MAKE. Refer to page 98 for a list of common options. The list of options supported by your system may be much longer.

MAKE runs a separate process for each command line in the makefile. Therefore, if we want to change directories and issue a command to take effect in the new directory, we must remember to place both commands on a single logical command line in the makefile and to separate the commands with a semicolon (;).

Because MAKE reads environment variables before reading the makefile, we can redefine an environment variable by assigning a new value to it in the makefile. The environment variable `MAKEFLAGS` remembers input options; MAKE uses the options stored in `MAKEFLAGS` when we apply the recursion process to MAKE.

From highest (1) to lowest (4), the order of precedence for macros in MAKE is:

1. macros defined on the command line

2. macros defined in the makefile

3. macros defined in the system environment

4. macros predefined by the system

The UNIX system's MAKE supports more predefined macros, knows more suffixes, and has more inference rules than the DOS versions of MAKE. Two predefined macros unique to MAKE on UNIX systems are **LEX** and **YACC**. Also unique is the *null suffix* exemplified by the **.c:** inference rule, which MAKE uses to build an executable file from a **.c** file.

We can display the values of all predefined macros, inference rules, and environment variables known to MAKE by using the **p** option.

Appendix A

Comparing MAKE

Feature	Microsoft's NMAKE	Borland's MAKE	UNIX System's MAKE
name	`nmake`	`make`	`make`
macros			
user-defined	yes	yes	yes
predefined	yes	no	yes
inference rules			
user-defined	yes	yes	yes
predefined	yes	no	yes
pseudotargets			
user-defined	yes	yes	yes
predefined	yes	yes[a]	yes
in-line files	yes	yes	no
directives	yes	yes	no
information file	`tools.ini`	`builtins.mak`	—
precede commands	with space(s) or tab(s)		with tab(s)

[a]Predefined pseudotargets are called *dot directives* in Borland's MAKE.

Appendix B

Microsoft's NMAKE

This is a summary of the built-in items for NMAKE that are used and described in this book. Refer to the documentation from Microsoft for more details and additions to these lists.

Command Line

    nmake [options] [macros] [targets]

- Arguments enclosed in [ ] are optional

- The command line entry is case sensitive

Options

a	i	s
c	n	t
d	nologo	x *filename*
e	p	z
f *filename*	q	?
help	r	

- Precede options with – or /

- Options are not case sensitive

- *filename* arguments (to options f and x) are not case sensitive

Predefined Macros

$@	current target
$*	base filename with path
$<	full filename with path
CC	C compiler (cl)
CFLAGS	empty macro
AS	assembler (masm)
AFLAGS	empty macro
MAKE	NMAKE command (nmake)

- All predefined and user-defined macros are case sensitive

Predefined Inference Rules

```
.c.obj:
        $(CC)   $(CFLAGS)   -c $*.c


.asm.obj:
        $(AS)   $(AFLAGS)   $*.c ;


.c.exe:
        $(CC)   $(CFLAGS)   $*.c
```

Predefined Pseudotargets

```
.SILENT:
.IGNORE:
.SUFFIXES:   .asm  .c  .obj  .exe
```

- All predefined pseudotargets are case sensitive; user-defined pseudotargets are not

Preprocessing Directives

cmdswitches	if *expr*	else
error *message*	ifdef *name*	endif
include <*filename*>	ifndef *name*	undef *name*
include "*filename*"		

- Precede with ! (left justified; no spaces or tabs)

- Directives are not case sensitive

Special Characters

comment	#
escape control character	^
line continuation indicator	\
in-line file delimiters	<<*filename*
	⋮
	<<
or	
	<<*filename*
	⋮
	<<keep

- the ending << and <<nokeep are equivalent

Appendix C

Borland's MAKE

This is a summary of the built-in items for MAKE that are used and described in this book. Refer to the documentation from Borland for more details and additions to these lists.

Command Line

    make [options] [targets]

- Arguments enclosed in [ ] are optional

- The command line entry is case sensitive

Options

a	h	s
B	i	S
D*identifier*	I*directory*	U*identifier*
D*identifier=string*	K	W
f*filename*	n	?

- Precede options with - or /

- No space between option and argument

- Options and option arguments are case sensitive; except *filename* argument to option f is not case sensitive

Predefined Macros

$*	base filename with path
$<	full filename with path
$d	defined test macro

Predefined Inference Rules

- none (user-defined inference rules *are* supported)

Dot Directives (Predefined Pseudotargets)

```
.SILENT:
.IGNORE:
```

- All predefined pseudotargets are case sensitive; user-defined pseudotargets are not

Preprocessing Directives

if *expr*	error *message*
elif *expr*	include "*filename*"
else	undef *name*
endif	

- Precede with ! (left justified; no spaces or tabs)

- Directives are not case sensitive

- Arguments to directives are case sensitive

Special Characters

comment	#
line continuation indicator	\
in-line file delimiters	<<!
	⋮
	!

Appendix D

UNIX System's MAKE

This is a summary of the built-in items for MAKE that are used and described in this book. Refer to the online manual page for MAKE for more details and additions to these lists.

Command Line

    make [options] [macros] [targets]

- Arguments enclosed in [ ] are optional

- The command line entry is case sensitive

Options

d	n	r
e	p	s
f *filename*	q	t
i		

- Precede options with -

- Options and option arguments are case sensitive

Predefined Macros

`$@`	current target
`$*`	base filename with path
`$<`	full filename with path
`CC`	C compiler (`cc`)
`CFLAGS`	empty macro
`AS`	assembler (`as`)
`ASFLAGS`	empty macro
`MAKE`	MAKE command (`make`)

- All predefined and user-defined macros are case sensitive

Predefined Inference Rules

```
.c.obj:
        $(CC) $(CFLAGS) -c $<
.s.o:
        $(AS) $(ASFLAGS) -o $@ $<
.c:
        $(CC) $(CFLAGS) $(LDFLAGS) $< -o $@
```

Predefined Pseudotargets

```
.SILENT:
.IGNORE:
.SUFFIXES: .s  .c  .o
```

- All predefined and user-defined pseudotargets are case sensitive

Preprocessing Directives

- none

Special Characters

comment	`#`
line continuation indicator	`\`

Appendix E

Depends Utility

Purpose

Generate dependency list for the `.obj` files that appear in a DOS makefile.

Syntax

    depends -IPath [-IPath ...] [-ffilename] [-Q]

    depends -I Path [-I Path ...] [-f filename] [-Q]

Description

The `depends` program reads a makefile and collects the `.obj` names in a dependency list. It then reads the source file for the corresponding `.obj` file in the dependency list looking for `include` files. `depends` handles `.c` and `.asm` source files. For each `include` file, `depends` searches the path(s) indicated with the `I` option(s) for an occurrence of the `include` file and produces a dependency line for the makefile.

The output from the program goes to `stdout` (the standard output in DOS is the screen).

Here are the options that the program supports:

- **-f** *filename* or **-f***filename*
  The name of the makefile to be parsed. The default name is `makefile.old`.

- **-I** *includepath* or **-I***includepath*
  The path where `depends` searches for `include` files. There is *no*

default path so you must specify at least one I; the maximum number of Is is 10.

- **-Q**
  Converts all relative paths to fully qualified paths.

You can use a dash (−) in front of an option, as we show above, or a slash (/) if you prefer the DOS style for parameters. The order of options is *not* important.

Examples

```
depends  -I. -I\c\include >makefile
```

depends will search the current directory (.) and **\c\include** for the include files. The input file is the default **makefile.old**. The output will be written to the file **makefile**.

Notice that the **−I** and **−f** options can have their arguments next to them or separated by blanks or tabs. For example,

```
depends  -I. -I\c\include >makefile
```

and

```
depends  -I . -I \c\include >makefile
```

are equivalent.

In the next example,

```
depend -f temp.mak -I. -I..\c\include -Q >makefile
```

depends will read the makefile **temp.mak**; it will then search . and **..\c\include** directories; and it will produce fully qualified dependency paths because of **−Q**. The output will be written to **makefile**.

```
depend -f temp.mak -I. -I%INCLUDE% -Q >makefile
```

depends will read the makefile **temp.mak**; it will then search . and the directories listed in the environment variable INCLUDE; and it will produce fully qualified dependency paths because of **−Q**. The output will be written to **makefile**. Note that when we use NMAKE and invoke **depends** from the makefile, we need to add an extra pair of %s around the environment variable INCLUDE because % is a special character in NMAKE. The example above becomes:

```
depend -f temp.mak -I. -I%%INCLUDE%% -Q >makefile
```

Note: It is important that you do *not* redirect the output to the file that is also the input to depends. For example, this is an *error*:

```
depend  -I.  -f tmpfile  >tmpfile
```

The DOS shell will open `tmpfile` for output and will truncate the size of an existing file to zero before depends has the chance to read `tmpfile`.

Observations

More sophisticated dependency tools may be available on your system. Some versions of *make*, like Borland's MAKE, have dependency analysis built in. Consult your local guru.

Outline for the depends Utility

```
handle command line arguments

Scan() - scan the input file for .obj
    Dependencies() - find xxx.obj names
        AddRecord() - add xxx.obj to the list of
                        .obj names

ScanFile() - for each xxx.obj in the list
    is there a xxx.c file?
        ScanC()
            search for '#include'
            search the -I directories for the file name
                following the '#include'
            output a dependency line for the file name
    or is there a xxx.asm file?
        ScanAsm()
            search for 'include'
            search the -I directories for the file name
                following the 'include'
            output a dependency line for the file name
```

```
//
//   Program Name: depends
//
//   Description:
//     This program creates a set of dependencies for
//     assembler and C programs.
//     The input is a valid makefile. The output is the
//     original file plus the list of dependencies.
//     The output is written to stdout.
//
//   Compiler:         Microsoft C Version 6.0A
//   Operating System: DOS

//   Include Files

#include        <stdio.h>
#include        <string.h>
#include        <stdlib.h>
#include        <ctype.h>
#include        <direct.h>
#include        <dos.h>

//   Symbolic Constants

#define     FAIL            1
#define     MAXFILENAME     15
#define     MAXINCPATHS     10
#define     MAXLINE         100
#define     NO              0
#define     YES             1

#define     FIND            _dos_findfirst

//   Function Prototypes

int     main        (int argc, char *argv[]);
void    AddRecord   (char *src);
void    Dependencies (char *line);
void    Error       (char *message);
```

```
int     GetFile         (int argc, char *argv[], int cnt);
int     GetPath         (int argc, char *argv[], int cnt);
void    *GetMemory      (unsigned nbytes);
void    IncPathsCnt     (int *IncCnt);
void    Scan            (FILE *fileptr);
void    ScanAsm         (FILE *fileptr, char *filename);
void    ScanC           (FILE *fileptr, char *filename);
void    ScanFile        (struct target *Targets);
void    SearchPaths     (char *iname);
void    Usage           (void);

// Global Variables

char    FileName[MAXFILENAME],
        *IncPaths[MAXINCPATHS],
        NewFilename[MAXFILENAME];

int     IncCnt = -1,     // total number of include paths
        NeedContinuation = NO,
        Qflags = NO;     // do not use fully qualified paths

struct target
{
        char            *name;
        struct target   *next;
};

struct target *TargetsBegin, *TargetsEnd;

// main: main function for 'depends'
int main (int argc, char *argv[])
{
    char    line[MAXLINE],
            *ptr;
    int     cnt;         // argument count
    FILE    *fileptr;    // pointer to input file
```

```
                        // Initialize default file name
strcpy(FileName, "makefile.old");

if (argc < 2)           // Not enough arguments?
    Usage();
else                    // Check command line options
{
    for (cnt = 1; cnt < argc; cnt++)
    {
        if ( argv[cnt][0] != '-' &&
             argv[cnt][0] != '/')
        {
            sprintf(line, "Invalid Option ==> [ %s ]\n",
                                            argv[cnt]);
            Error(line);
            Usage();
        }
        else
        {
            switch(argv[cnt][1])
            {
                case 'i':
                case 'I':
                    // Get include path information
                    cnt = GetPath(argc, argv, cnt);
                    break;
                case 'f':
                case 'F':
                    // Get makefile name
                    cnt = GetFile(argc, argv, cnt);
                    break;
                case 'q':
                case 'Q':
                    // Use fully qualified paths
                    Qflags = YES;
                    break;
```

```
                    default:
                        sprintf(line,
                        "Invalid Option ==> [ %s ]\n",
                                            argv[cnt]);
                        Error(line);
                        Usage();
                        break;
                }
            }
        }
    }
    if (IncCnt < 0)            // need at least one -I
        Usage();
                                // Open input file
    if ((fileptr = fopen(FileName, "r")) == NULL)
    {
        sprintf(line,
                "Can't open file ==> [ %s ]\n", FileName);
        Error(line);
        exit(FAIL);
    }
    Scan(fileptr);             // Scan the input file
    fclose(fileptr);

    ScanFile(TargetsBegin); // Scan each source file
    return 0;
}
```

```
// AddRecord: add a new record (with file name) to list
void AddRecord(char *filename)
{
    register struct target *ptr;

    // Filename in the linked list?
    for (ptr = TargetsBegin; ptr; ptr = ptr->next)
    {
        if ( strcmp(ptr->name, filename ) == 0)
            return;  // Filename already in the list
    }
    // Get memory space for new node
    ptr = GetMemory(sizeof(struct target));

    // Add node to the linked list
    if (!TargetsEnd)     // The list is empty
        TargetsBegin = ptr;
    else                 // Add node to end of the list
        TargetsEnd->next = ptr;
    ptr->next  = NULL;
    ptr->name  = filename;
    TargetsEnd = ptr;
}
```

```
// Dependencies: find .obj file name and add it to the list
void  Dependencies(char *line)
{
    register char   *src = strdup(line);
    register char   *ptr;

    for (ptr = strstr(src, ".obj"); ptr;
         ptr = strstr(ptr, ".obj"))
    {
        // Mark the end of the file name
        *(ptr + 4) = '\0';

        // Back up to beginning of the file name
        for ( ; ptr >= src && !isspace(*ptr); ptr--)
            ;
        // add the file name to linked list of file names
        AddRecord(++ptr);

        // point past current file name
        ptr += strlen(ptr) + 1;
    }
}


// Error: display error message
void Error(char *message)
{
    fprintf(stderr, "%s", message);
}
```

```
// GetFile: get file name from the command line
int GetFile(int argc, char *argv[], int cnt)
{
    char    line[MAXLINE];  // local buffer

                                // -ffilename
    if (argv[cnt][2] != '\0')
        strcpy(FileName, &argv[cnt][2]);
    else
    {                               // -f  filename
        if (cnt+1 >= argc)
        {
            sprintf(line, "Missing Filename ==> [ %s ]\n",
                                                argv[cnt]);
            Error(line);
            Usage();
        }
        strcpy(FileName, argv[++cnt]);
    }
    return cnt;
}
```

```
// GetPath: get include path and environment variables
int GetPath(int argc, char *argv[], int cnt)
{
    char    line[MAXLINE],   // local buffer
            *endptr,
            *environ,        // pointer to environment var
            *ptr;            // pointer to include path

    if (argv[cnt][2] != '\0')
                             // -iincludepath
        ptr = &argv[cnt][2];
    else
    {                        // -i  includepath
        if (cnt+1 >= argc)
        {
            sprintf(line, "Missing Path ==> [ %s ]\n",
                                        argv[cnt]);
            Error(line);
            Usage();
        }
        ptr = &argv[++cnt][0];
    }

    if (*ptr != '%')         // include path
    {
        IncPathsCnt(&IncCnt);
        IncPaths[IncCnt] = GetMemory(strlen(ptr)+1);
        strcpy(IncPaths[IncCnt], ptr);
    }
```

```
    else                    // environment variable
    {
        if ((endptr = strstr(++ptr, "%")) == NULL)
        {
            sprintf(line, "Invalid Option ==> [ %s ]\n",
                                            argv[cnt]);
            Error(line);
            Usage();
        }
        else                // valid environment var
        {
            *endptr = '\0'; // terminate environment var
            strupr(ptr);
            if ((environ = getenv(ptr)) == NULL)
            {
                sprintf(line,
                  "Unknown environment variable ==> %s\n",
                                                environ);
                Error(line);
                exit(FAIL);
            }
            else            // parse environment
            {
                strcpy(line, environ);
                for (ptr = strtok(line, ";"); ptr;
                     ptr = strtok(NULL, ";"))
                {
                    IncPathsCnt(&IncCnt);
                    IncPaths[IncCnt] =
                                GetMemory(strlen(ptr)+1);
                    strcpy(IncPaths[IncCnt], ptr);
                }
            }
        }
    }
    return cnt;      // index of the last argument parsed
}
```

```
// GetMemory: get nbytes of memory
void *GetMemory(unsigned nbytes)
{
    char    *ptr = malloc(nbytes);

    if (!ptr)
    {
        Error("GetMemory: cannot allocate space\n");
        exit(FAIL);
    }
    return ptr ;
}


// IncPathsCnt: increment IncCnt and test upper limit
void IncPathsCnt(int *IncCnt)
{
    if (+++*IncCnt >= MAXINCPATHS)
    {
        Error("Too many include files...\n");
        Error("Program terminated.\n");
        exit(FAIL);
    }
}
```

```
// Scan: scan the input file for .obj discarding
//       .obj: and its continuation lines
void Scan(FILE *fileptr)
{
    char    line[MAXLINE];
    char    *ptr;

    while (fgets(line, MAXLINE, fileptr))
    {
        // Check for .obj in the line
        if (strstr(line, ".obj"))
        {
            if (strstr(line, ".c.obj")      ||
                strstr(line, ".asm.obj")    ||
                strstr(line, ".SUFFIXES"))
                ;       // Ignore suffixes and suffix rules
            else if (!strstr(line, ".obj:"))
                    // Collect .obj dependencies
                Dependencies(line);
            else        // It is .obj:; skip target
            {           // and continuation lines
                while ((ptr=strrchr(line, '\\')) != NULL)
                {
                    if (*(ptr+1) != '\n')
                        break;  // end of continuation
                    else if (!fgets(line, MAXLINE, fileptr))
                        break;  // end of file
                }
                // discard .obj: and continuation lines
                continue;
            }
        }
        fputs(line, stdout);
    }
    fputs("\n", stdout);
}
```

```
// ScanAsm: scan a .asm file for 'include' lines
void ScanAsm(FILE *fileptr, char *filename)
{
    char    line[MAXLINE],
            *ptr;

    // Print out file name
    fprintf(stdout, "%s", filename);
    NeedContinuation = YES;

    while (fgets(line, MAXLINE, fileptr))
    {
        if (strncmp(line, "include", 7) == 0)
        {
            ptr = strtok(line, "\t ");
            ptr = strtok(NULL, "\t ");
            SearchPaths(ptr);
        }
    }
    fprintf(stdout, "\n");
    NeedContinuation = NO;
}
```

```
// ScanC: scan a .c file for '#include' lines
void ScanC(FILE *fileptr, char *filename)
{
    char    line[MAXLINE],
            *ptr;

    // Print out file name and a continuation line
    fprintf(stdout, "%s", filename);
    NeedContinuation = YES;

    while (fgets(line, MAXLINE, fileptr))
    {
        if (strncmp(line, "#include", 8) == 0)
        {
            ptr = strtok(line, "\t\"< ");
            ptr = strtok(NULL, "\t\"<> ");
            SearchPaths(ptr);
        }
    }
    fprintf(stdout, "\n");
    NeedContinuation = NO;
}
```

```c
// ScanFile: scan linked list for names of target files
void ScanFile(struct target *head)
{
    register struct target  *ptr;
    register char           *q;
    FILE                    *fileptr;
    char filename[MAXFILENAME];

    for (ptr = TargetsBegin; ptr; ptr = ptr->next)
    {
        // Print target name; e.g.:  a.obj:
        fprintf(stdout, "%s: ", ptr->name);

        q = strchr(ptr->name, '.');
        *q = '\0';
        sprintf(filename, "%s.c", ptr->name);

        if ((fileptr = fopen(filename, "r")) != NULL)
        {
            ScanC(fileptr, filename);
            fclose(fileptr);
        }
        else
        {
            sprintf(filename, "%s.asm", ptr->name);
            if ((fileptr = fopen(filename, "r")) == NULL)
                fprintf(stderr, "Ignoring %s. . .\n",
                                            ptr->name);
            else
            {
                ScanAsm(fileptr, filename);
                fclose(fileptr);
            }
        }
    }
}
```

```c
// SearchPaths: search for include file and return its path
void SearchPaths(char *iname )
{
    char    line[MAXLINE],
            curpath[MAXLINE],
            newpath[MAXLINE];
    int     cnt;
    struct find_t   directory;

    for (cnt = 0; cnt <= IncCnt; cnt++)
    {
        sprintf(line, "%s\\%s", IncPaths[cnt], iname);
        if (FIND(line, _A_NORMAL, &directory) == 0)
        {
            if (Qflags == NO)    // do not use qualified path
            {
                if (NeedContinuation)
                    fprintf(stdout, "\t\\\n");
                fprintf(stdout, "\t\t%s\\%-15s",
                                    IncPaths[cnt], iname);
            }
            else                 // use fully qualified path
            {                    // get current directory
                getcwd(curpath, MAXLINE);
                                 // cd to include directory
                chdir(IncPaths[cnt]);
                                 // get qualified path
                getcwd(newpath, MAXLINE);
                                 // return to working dir.
                chdir(curpath);
                if (NeedContinuation)
                    fprintf(stdout, "\t\\\n");
                fprintf(stdout, "\t\t%s\\%-15s",
                                        newpath, iname);
            }
            break;               // found include directory
        }
    }
}
```

```c
// Usage: display usage message for 'depends'
void Usage(void)
{
    fprintf(stderr,
    "Usage: depends [options]\n"
    "        where each option can be any of the \n"
    "        following (in any order):\n"
    "           -f filename\n"
    "               name of the makefile to parse\n"
    "               (instead of 'makefile.old')\n"
    "           -I includepath\n"
    "               Include Path information\n"
    "               Minimum: one -I includepath\n"
    "               Maximum: 10  -I includepath\n"
    "           -Q  Produce fully qualified paths\n"
    "        All output goes to stdout\n");
    exit(FAIL);
}
```

Makefile for depends

```
CFLAGS  =  -W2  -O

depends.exe:    depends.obj
        $(CC)  -o  depends.exe  depends.obj
```

Index

! and Borland's MAKE   83, 95
! and in-line response   59
! and NMAKE   67, 79
! and `tlink`   59
! delimiter   59
! NOT operator   87, 95
comment indicator   3, 8
#, example of   35, 36
$( )   15, 20, 71, 87
$* predefined macro   24, 25, 31, 39
$< predefined macro   25, 29, 39, 102
$@ predefined macro   24, 32, 39
$d predefined macro   84, 86, 95
- option indicator   12, 66, 82, 98
`.asm.obj` inference rule   33
`.c.o` inference rule   34, 102
`.c.obj` inference rule   29, 33
`.c:` inference rule   102
`.com` file   102
`.exe` file   7, 102
`.h` files   73, 80, 91, 96
`.IGNORE:` pseudotarget   27, 40
`.inc` files   73, 80, 91, 96
`.o` files in UNIX   34, 102
`.obj` files   7, 102
`.s.o` inference rule   102
`.SILENT:` pseudotarget   27, 40
`.SUFFIXES:` pseudotarget   27, 40, 61, 101

/ option indicator   12, 66, 82
// comments in C   119
~ in extensions   102
: on a target line   3
<< and in-line response   59
<< and `link`   58, 59
? option   66, 82
@ and in-line response   58, 59
@ and `link`   57, 58
@ and `tlink`   59
\ and ^   73
\ continuation character   3, 8, 72, 90, 99
\, example of   35, 36
\\ in Borland's   90, 95
^ and \   72
^ caret   73

a option   66, 82, 93, 96
advantages of macros   20
AFLAGS macro   33
AS macro   33
autoresponse file, `link`   57
autoresponse file, `tlink`   59

B option   82
backslash (\)   3, 72
Borland's \\   90, 95
Borland's C compiler   7, 14

Borland's f option   12, 20, 60
Borland's MAKE   23, 24, 111
Borland's MAKE and !   83, 95
Borland's MAKE options   82
Borland's tcc   7, 14
built-in macro $*   24, 25, 31
built-in macro $<   25, 29
built-in macro $@   24, 32
built-in macros   22
builtins.mak file   81, 93, 96

C compiler (cc)   16
C compiler (cl)   7
C compiler (tcc)   7
C compiler, Borland's   7
C compiler, Microsoft's   7
C compiler, UNIX system's   16
C files in UNIX   34
c option   66, 102
caret ^   73
cc command   16, 24, 39
CC macro   15, 16, 39
CC predefined macro   23, 24, 39
CFLAGS empty   33
CFLAGS macro   15, 16
changing directories   44, 46, 98
cl command   7, 14, 23, 39, 56
cl, linking using   56
code, return   27
command, implicit   29, 40
command line indentation   2, 8
command line indentation, DOS   3
command line indentation, UNIX   3
command line macro   47, 49
commands and dependency   20
commands and spaces   98
commands and tabs   98

commands and targets   5, 13
commands, explicit   5
commands, hard-coded   13, 14, 20
commands with macros   14
comment in C and //   119
comment indicator #   3, 8
common errors   59
continuation character \   3, 8, 72, 90, 99
continuation lines   3, 72, 90
creating an environment variable   52
current target macro   24, 25
current target, synonym for   24
current target without an extension   25

D option   49, 82, 86, 95
d option   66, 98
date and time   7
default target   4
dependencies   5, 8, 17
dependencies, example of   14
dependency and commands   20
dependency, direct   5
dependency example, direct   5, 47
dependency example, indirect   5
dependency, indirect   5
dependency tree   6, 18, 19
depends utility   75, 115
direct dependency   5
direct dependency example   5, 47
directive, elif   83, 95
directive, if   70, 83, 95
directive, if...else   70, 83, 86, 95

directive, `ifdef`   69, 71
directive, `include`   68, 83
directive, nested `if`   88
directive, `undef`   83
directives, dot   27, 40
directories, changing   44, 46, 98
DOS command line indentation   3
dot directives   27, 40

`e` option   56, 66, 98
`elif` directive   83, 95
empty `CFLAGS`   33
empty macro   33
environment variable   51, 52, 53, 71
environment variable, creating an   52
error messages   59
errors, example of   59
example of makefile   2, 16, 22, 25, 32, 35, 38, 44, 46, 48, 50
executable files in UNIX   34
explicit commands   5
extension, file name   28
extensions and ~   102

`f` option   12, 13, 19, 60, 66, 82, 98
`f` option, Borland's   12, 20, 60
file name extension   28
file name suffix   28
file names and macros   47
files, .obj   7
files in SCCS   102
files, UNIX   34

first makefile   2
first target   4
first target, making the   12

`h` option   82
hard-coded commands   13, 14, 20
header files   73, 80

`I` option   82
`i` option   27, 40, 66, 82, 98
`if` directive   70, 83, 95
`if` directive, nested   88
`if...else` directive   70, 83, 86, 95
`if...else` example   70, 71
`if[...]` example   71
`ifdef` directive   69, 71
implicit command   29, 40
implicit target   29, 40
in-line response and !   59
in-line response and <<   59
in-line response and @   58, 59
in-line response, `link`   58
`include` directive   68, 83
include files   73, 80
indenting command lines   2, 8
indirect dependency   5
indirect dependency example   5
inference rule .asm.obj   33
inference rule .c.o   34, 102
inference rule .c.obj   29, 33
inference rule .c: 102
inference rule .s.o   102
inference rule, predefined   33, 102
inference rule, user-defined   31, 40

inference rules   4, 28, 29, 31, 40
INIT environment variable   78
input file, link   57
input file, tlink   59
invoking *make*   4, 6, 8, 11, 107,
      111, 113
invoking *make* recursively   43
invoking *make* with a target   4, 9
invoking Borland's MAKE   81
invoking NMAKE   65, 107
invoking UNIX MAKE   97

K option   59, 82, 93

link and <<   58, 59
link and @   57, 58
link autoresponse file   57
link command   56
link in-line response   58
link input file   57
link, linking using   57
link response file   57
linking using cl   56
linking using link   57
linking using tlink   59

macro AFLAGS   33
macro AS   33
macro CC   15, 16, 39
macro CFLAGS   15, 16
macro, current target   24, 25
macro, empty   33
macro names   21
macro on the command line   47,
      49

macro, using a   15
macro, value of a   15, 20, 71, 87
macro, what is a   15
macros   20
macros, advantages of using   16,
      20
macros and $()   15
macros and file names   47
macros, built-in   22
macros, commands with   14
macros, precedence of   80, 96, 103
macros, predefined   22, 23, 30, 38
macros, printing   12
macros, user-defined   22, 23, 38
macros, value of *make*   26
make and recursion   43, 45
MAKE, Borland's   1, 23, 24, 111
make, invoking   4, 6, 8, 11, 107,
      111, 113
make, invoking with a target   4
make options   11, 12, 82, 98
MAKE predefined macro   44, 63,
      76, 100
make, re-invoking   46, 47
make, specifying file name   12
make, the theory   2
MAKE, UNIX system's   23, 24,
      97, 113
makefile   1, 12, 13
makefile example   2, 16, 22, 25,
      32, 35, 38, 44, 46, 48, 50
makefile, first   2
makefile name   12
makefile, renaming a   12
MAKEFLAGS predefined macro   99,
      103
making the first target   12
Microsoft's C compiler   7
Microsoft's cl   7

Microsoft's NMAKE   23, 33, 107

n option   12, 13, 19, 26, 39, 66, 82, 98, 100
name for a makefile   12
nested if directives   88
NMAKE   23
NMAKE and !   67, 79
NMAKE, invoking   65, 107
NMAKE, Microsoft's   1, 23, 33, 107
NMAKE options   66
NMAKE, preprocessing directives in   67
NOT operator !   87, 95
null suffix rule   102

object files in UNIX   34
option ?   66, 82
option a   66, 82, 93, 96
option B   82
option c   66, 102
option D   49, 82, 86, 95
option d   66, 98
option e   56, 66, 98
option f   12, 13, 19, 60, 66, 82, 98
option f, Borland's   12, 20, 60
option h   82
option I   82
option i   27, 40, 66, 82, 98
option indicator (-)   12, 66, 82, 98
option indicator (/)   12, 66, 82
option K   59, 82, 93
option n   12, 13, 19, 26, 39, 66, 82, 98, 100

option p   12, 26, 35, 39, 66, 98, 100, 103
option q   66, 98
option r   66, 98
option S   82
option s   27, 40, 66, 82, 98
option t   66, 98
option U   82
option W   82
option x   66
options, make   11, 12
options, Borland's MAKE   82
options, NMAKE   66
options, order of   13, 20
options, UNIX MAKE   98
order of options   13, 20

p option   12, 26, 35, 39, 66, 98, 100, 103
placement, target/dependency line   2
position of a target   20
pound sign (#)   3
precedence of macros   80, 96, 103
predefined inference rule   33, 102
predefined macro $*   24, 25, 31, 39
predefined macro $<   25, 29, 39, 102
predefined macro $@   24, 32, 39
predefined macro $d   84, 86, 95
predefined macro CC   23, 24
predefined macro MAKE   44, 63, 76, 100
predefined macro MAKEFLAGS   99, 103
predefined macros   22, 23, 30, 38
predefined pseudotargets   27, 40

preprocessing directives in MAKE
    83
preprocessing directives in NMAKE
    67
printing macros   12
program `depends`   75, 115
pseudotarget `.IGNORE:`   27, 40
pseudotarget `.SILENT:`   27, 40
pseudotarget `.SUFFIXES:`   27, 40,
    61, 101
pseudotargets   26, 39, 45, 77
pseudotargets, predefined   27, 40
pseudotargets, user-defined   26,
    39

`q` option   66, 98

`r` option   66, 98
re-invoking *make*   46, 47
readability   3, 67, 83
recursion and *make*   43, 45
renaming a makefile   12
response and `<<`, in-line   59
response and `@`, in-line   58, 59
response file, `link`   57
response file, `tlink`   59
response, `link` in-line   58
response, `tlink` in-line   59
return code   27
rules, inference   28, 29, 31, 40
rules, suffix   28, 40

`S` option   82
`s` option   27, 40, 66, 82, 98
SCCS files   102

`set` command   51, 72
spaces and commands   98
specifying a target   19
specifying file name in *make*   12
suffix, file name   28
suffix, null   102
suffix rules   4, 28, 29, 40
synonym for current target   24
synonym for target without exten-
    sion   24
syntax rules   2

`t` option   66, 98
tabs and commands   98
target, default   4
target, example of   4, 14, 24
target, implicit   29, 40
target line and `:`   3
target macro, current   24
target, position of a   20
target, specifying a   19
target, the first   4
target, what is   3
target without an extension   24
target without extension, synonym
    for   24
target/dependency line placement
    2
targets and commands   5, 13
`tcc` command   7, 14
theory of *make*   2
time and date   7
time stamp   2, 7, 8
`tlink` and `!`   59
`tlink` and `@`   59
`tlink` command   59
`tlink` input file   59
`tools.ini` file   65

tree, dependency   6, 18

U option   82
undef directive   83
UNIX, .o files in   34, 102
UNIX, C files in   34
UNIX, executable files in   34
UNIX files   34
UNIX MAKE, example of   50
UNIX MAKE options   98
UNIX, object files in   34
UNIX system's *make*   23, 24, 97, 113
UNIX systems command line in-dentation   3
up-to-date files   7
user-defined inference rules   31, 40
user-defined macros   22, 23, 38
user-defined pseudotargets   26, 39
using a macro   15
using **set**   51, 72
utility depends   75, 115

value of *make* macros   26
value of a macro   15, 20, 71, 87
variable, environment   51, 52, 53

W option   82

x option   66